Re-visioning Medusa:
from Monster to Divine Wisdom

a Girl God Anthology

Edited by Glenys Livingstone, Ph.D.,

Trista Hendren and Pat Daly

Preface by Joan Marler

Cover Art by Arna Baartz

©2017 All Rights Reserved

Updated October 2024

ISBN: 9781544179650

All writings and art are the property of individual contributors. All rights reserved. None of the writings or artwork herein may be reproduced or utilized in any form or by any means, electronic or mechanical, including photocopying, recording or by any information storage and retrieval system, without prior written permission from the author or artist.

www.thegirlgod.com

Praise for Re-visioning Medusa

"I welcome *Re-visioning Medusa: from Monster to Divine Wisdom* wholeheartedly. Medusa unfolds the original vision of the female divine. Calling her a rebel underestimates her power. In short, the symbol of Medusa embodies Goddess Feminism, Activism, and Spirituality. Together with women, Medusa is ever present in the intergalactic journey of the Great Goddess."
-Helen Hye-Sook Hwang, Ph.D., author of *The Mago Way*

"No better time than now to be Re-visioning Medusa! Let's take her off the shelf, dust her off and embrace her! No more enduring, being docile, being quiet for others comfort. It's time to embrace our strength, our courage, our agency—even our rage!"
-Karen Tate, author, speaker, social justice activist and radio show host of *Voices of the Sacred Feminine*

"I am in awe of this powerful anthology! The *Re-visioning Medusa* Anthology looks at the myth and medicine of Medusa in a whole new light shining her much needed ancient wisdom back into the world. This deeper insight into her stories and magic is a compelling reclaiming of feminine fire. A must read!"
-Ara Campbell, *The Goddess Circle*

"Who was the mythical Medusa? The original "nasty woman," ugly and fearsome? Or the inspiring feminist model of a fearless woman daring to speak truth to male power? This fascinating collection both asks and answers this timely question."
-Donna Henes, author of *The Queen of My Self*

"An exceptional anthology, Re-visioning Medusa will be valued not only by people who have studied and worked with Medusa for some time, but also those who haven't yet wondered about Her."
-Judith Laura, author of *Goddess Matters: the Mystical, Practical, & Controversial*

www.thegirlgod.com

Girl God Books

Inanna's Ascent: Reclaiming Female Power
An anthology examining how women can rise from the underworld and reclaim their power. All contributors are extraordinary women in their own right, who have been through some difficult life lessons—and are bravely share their stories.

In Defiance of Oppression - The Legacy of Boudicca
An anthology that encapsulates the Spirit of the defiant warrior in a modern apathetic age. No longer will the voices of our sisters go unheard, as the ancient Goddesses return to the battlements, calling to ignite the spark within each and every one of us—to defy oppression wherever we find it, and stand together in solidarity.

Warrior Queen: Answering the Call of The Morrigan
A powerful anthology about the Irish Celtic Goddess. Each contributor brings The Morrigan to life with unique stories that invite readers to partake and inspire them to pen their own. Included are essays, poems, stories, chants, rituals, and art from dozens of story-tellers and artists from around the world, illustrating and recounting the many ways this powerful Goddess of war, death, and prophecy has changed their lives.

On the Wings of Isis: Reclaiming the Sovereignty of Auset
For centuries, women have lived, fought and died for their equality, independence and sovereignty. Originally known as Auset, the Egyptian Goddess Isis reveals such a path. Unfurl your wings and join an array of strong women who have embodied the Goddess of Ten Thousand Names to celebrate their authentic selves.

How to Live Well Despite Capitalist Patriarchy
A book challenging societal assumptions to help women become stronger and break free of their chains.

Songs of Solstice: Goddess Carols
This Songbook celebrates the cycles of Nature—Birth, Life, and Death—through the changing Seasons (the Turning of the Wheel) from Autumn's abundance, for which we give thanks, to Winter's 'Dead Time,' when even the warmth of the Sun leaves us, and the world goes dark and cold. It is a celebration of both the Light and the Dark, since both are Sacred and both are needed for new Life to grow and flourish.

The Crone Initiation: Women Speak on the Menopause Journey
The Crone Initiation is an anthology of women's experiences of perimenopause and menopause, and the part Goddess plays in this journey. Crone's presence in the breakdowns and breakthroughs, the disintegration and rebuilding, is expressed through words and art. Meaning is reclaimed and the power of the Elder restored.

New Love: a reprogramming toolbox for undoing the knots
A powerful combination of emotional/spiritual techniques, art and inspiring words for women who wish to move away from patriarchal thought.

The Girl God
A book for children young and old, celebrating the Divine Female. Magically illustrated by Elisabeth Slettnes with quotes from various faith traditions and feminist thinkers.

My Name is Medusa
The story of the greatly misunderstood Goddess, including why she likes snakes. *My Name is Medusa* explores the "scary" dark side, the potency of nature and the importance of dreams. Arna Baartz gorgeously illustrates this tale by Glenys Livingstone, teaching children (big and small) that our power often lies in what we have been taught to fear and revile.

thegirlgod.com

Table of Contents

Preface   1
Joan Marler

A Note About Medusa's Language   7
Trista Hendren

Mother Medusa: Regenerative One   9

Glenys Livingstone, Ph.D.

Ceremonial Headpiece Invoking Ancient Medusa   17
Glenys Livingstone, Ph.D.

Yew Medusa   18
Cristina Biaggi, Ph.D.

Medusa: Ferocious and Beautiful, Petrifying and Healing: Through the Words of the Ancients   19
Miriam Robbins Dexter, Ph.D.

The Gorgon Medusa   48
Sudie Rakusin

What Happened to You, Medusa?   49
Barbara Ardinger, Ph.D.

Ave Medusa   50
Jeanne K. Raines

Medusa: When the Soldiers   51
Susan Hawthorne

Raging Medusa 52
Cristina Biaggi, Ph.D.

Calling Medusa In 53
Jane Meredith

Power 59
Lizzie Yee

To Stand Witness 60
Teri Uktena

See No Evil 63
Caroline Alkonost

Medusa: The Invitation 64
Maureen Owen

Oracle 75
Janet Guastavino

Sisterhood is Subversive 76
Diane Goldie

Medusa's Nappy Dreads 78
Luisah Teish

Fearless Protector: a Self-Portrait 79
Alyscia Cunningham

Till We Have Bodies 80
Kaalii Cargill, Ph.D.

Medusa, Athena, Sophia: 87
the Fierceness of Wisdom Justice
Bonnie Odiorne, AW, Ph.D.

Black Medusa   94
Cristina Biaggi, Ph.D.

Red Medusa   95
Cristina Biaggi, Ph.D.

Marija K.   96
Jack K. Jeansonne

Those Who Do Not Fear   97
Marija Krstic

Medusa's Hairdresser   98
Penny-Anne Beaudoin

Medusa   100
Susan Hawthorne

Medusa, My Mother and Me   101
Barbara C. Daughter

My Name is Medusa   107
Arna Baartz

Medusa Goddess: Up Close and Personal   108
Marie Summerwood

Sicilian Tambourine   112
Susan Hawthorne

Baubo 113
Susan Hawthorne

Medusa's Hall of Mirrors 114
Leslene della-Madre

Pythic Portals 127
Nuit Moore

Pegasus as a Symbol of Transcendence 134
Arna Baartz

Ancient Wisdom for Modern Times 135
C. Loran Hills

Medusa on Big Tree 142
Glenys Livingstone, Ph.D.

How You Can Reattach Medusa's Head 144
Marguerite Rigoglioso, Ph.D.

Medusa's Vindication (it will be the mirror) 148
Kerryn Coombs-Valeontis

Medusa's Mask (shield) of Righteous Rage 150
Kerryn Coombs-Valeontis

Medusa's Mask of Righteous Rage 151
Kerryn Coombs-Valeontis

Winged Beast 152
Caroline Alkonost

Medusa: Wisdom of the Crone Moon   153
Theresa Curtis, Ph.D.

Medusa Resume   162
Marie Summerwood

Medusa's Stunning Powers Reflected in Literature   163
Dr. Gillian M.E.(dusa) Alban

Kahlo Medusa   176
Meg Dreyer

Making Amends with Medusa   177
Dawn Glinski

Snakes Aren't Mean!   182
Arna Baartz

Mother Medusa   183
Elizabeth Oakes, Ph.D.

The Medusa Imaginal   185
Pegi Eyers

Re-visioning Medusa: A Personal Odyssey   188
Sara Wright

Adorations For Medusa   196
Rev. Angela Kunschmann

Museo Massimo   197
Susan Hawthorne

Medusa and Athena: 198
Ancient Allies in Healing Women's Trauma
Laura Shannon

Medusa Self-Portrait   214
Liliana Kleiner, Ph.D.

Re-stor(y)ing Sanity   215
Trista Hendren

Medusa Colouring Sheet   227
Arna Baartz

List of Contributors   239

Upcoming Titles from Girl God Books   246

Preface

Joan Marler

The remarkable anthology you are holding in your hands contains the personal stories, scholarly research, revelations, and original artwork by women from Australia, North America, Europe, Israel and Turkey. These offerings reflect the indelible presence of the Gorgon Medusa who has stimulated each author's unique journey of discovery. Who is this Medusa whose visage has haunted the western imagination for 2700 years? Why has she remained so potent, and why is it necessary to "re-vision" her now in the 21st century?

In the *Odyssey* (11.633-35) by the Greek poet Homer (c. 750 BCE), the hero Odysseus expresses his fear of encountering the Gorgon—a ghastly apparition, the threshold guardian of Hades. In Homer's *Iliad* (11.33-37), the ferocious face of the Gorgon is centrally placed on the kingly shield of Agamemnon to frighten his enemies. The Greek term *gorgos*—meaning "terrible," "frightful"—was used to designate the ultimate female monster.

According to Greek mythology, Medusa is a Triple Goddess, one of three gorgon sisters—Sthenno, Euryale, and Medusa—representing past, present, and future. Only Medusa exists as mortal in present time. Her complex lineage composed of multiple myths and stories, combined with cross-cultural influences, is masterfully presented in this volume by the linguist and archaeomythologist Miriam Robbins Dexter. She rightly points out that the typical emphasis on Medusa's fearsome features are the result of extreme Greek bias against female powers, which masks her life-giving and regenerative capacities.

Long before the Gorgon Medusa constellated within the archaic Greek world and was demonized as ugly and ultimately monstrous—with her tongue lolling between sharp fangs, with writhing serpents for hair and glaring eyes—the roots of her multi-layered iconography extended deep into pre-Greek cultures. The earliest agrarian societies of Southeastern Europe, from the 7th-4th millennia BCE, were intimately bonded with the seasonal realities of the living Earth. These egalitarian farmers who developed long-lived, sustainable societies understood that life feeds on life. Death and decomposition are inevitable consequences of being alive, and the nutrients released from previously living matter are essential for life's renewal. Within this context, concepts of the sacred are analogous to the cyclic continuity of all existence. In mythic terms, the Great Goddess, as the Sacred Source of all life, is a metaphor for life giving birth to itself and absorbing itself in death. Therefore, the Goddess of Life is also the Goddess of Death who is responsible for regeneration.[1] Goddesses in various guises who represent this eternal cycle are found in ancient traditions throughout the world. The nature of every society is shaped by prevailing attitudes—honoring and respectful, or fearful and antagonistic—concerning the humbling and unavoidable fact of our individual mortality.

Linguistic and archaeological evidence indicates that the Greeks developed from tribes of Indo-European speakers who began entering the Balkan peninsula most likely during the late 3rd millennium BCE. A gradual amalgamation took place between two contrasting social and ideological systems: the matrifocal Old European horticulturalists who venerated the deities of the Earth and the newcomers who brought an androcratic social structure, warfare, and the worship of sky gods.[2]

---

[1] Marija Gimbutas emphasized the significance of regeneration, without which all life would cease. For a presentation of Old European iconography related to the life-giving, death-wielding, and regenerative cycles, see Gimbutas, Marija. *The Language of the Goddess.* San Francisco: Harper San Francisco, 1989.
[2] Gimbutas, Marija. *The Civilization of the Goddess.* San Francisco: Harper SanFrancisco, 1991. See also: Marler, Joan. "An Archaeological Investigation of the Gorgon." *Re-Vision* (summer 2002): 15-23.

The establishment of the Greek patriarchal world shifted the previous cultural valence from the egalitarian continuity of the Old Religion to the extreme imposition of male dominance and the cult of the hero. Under this new world order, all challenges to male hegemonic systems were to be crushed. As the classicist Eva Keuls emphasizes, "the suppression of women, the military expansionism and the harshness in the conduct of civic affairs all sprang from a common aggressive impulse." That impulse was the expression of "male supremacy and the cult of power and violence."[3]

It is no surprise, then, that the earth deities of the Old Religion were demonized or co-opted. A typical task for Greek heroes was to rid the civilized world of those "earth-born bogeys."[4] The Gorgon Medusa, whose gaze turned men to stone, became an obvious target. Nevertheless, on the periphery of the Greek world, there is evidence that She was venerated in her ancient powers. During the 6th century BCE on the island of Corfu, a nine-foot-high full-bodied sculpture of Medusa was placed at the highest point on the pediment of the temple of Artemis.[5] This Medusa is not raging, but is radiant in her full potency. Snakes with open jaws extend from each side of her head and two copulating serpents encircle her waist, carrying the potential for both death and new life. She wears winged sandals, her great wings are fully extended, sheltering her two children, and her bent-knee posture suggests that she is flying. All shamanic dimensions are Hers—the Great Above, the Great Below, the Primordial Waters, and the entire expanse of the Earth. She is flanked by great felines, just as the Phrygian Mountain Goddess Cybele and the seated Ancestral Mother from Çatalhöyük before her.

---

[3] Keuls, Eva C. *The Reign of the Phallus: Sexual Politics in Ancient Athens.* Berkeley and Los Angeles: University of California Press, 1985:13.
[4] Harrison, Jane E. *Prolegomena to the Study of Greek Religion.* New York: Meridian Books, 1955: 162.
[5] See page 38.

The decapitation of Medusa by the Greek hero Perseus, assisted by the patriarchalized Goddess Athena, was painted on pottery, carved as bas reliefs on temples, described in Greek verse, and propagated in myths and legends. Her murder functioned as a cautionary tale defining the ultimate consequence of manifesting female sovereignty.

When Medusa was killed, her powers were plundered. She was pregnant with her son Chrysaor and the winged horse Pegasus who were born from her severed neck. Pegasus was immediately captured and made to bring Zeus Medusa's roar and the flash of her eyes, which he used as his thunder and lightning. In book three of the *Bibliotheca* (3.10.3) Apollodorus describes how Athena drains the blood from Medusa's veins and gives it to Asclepius, Greek god of medicine and healing. The blood from her left side is deadly poisonous, while the blood from her right side brings life. Asclepius's powers to cure and raise the dead were thereby stolen from Medusa.

Athena placed the apotropaic image of Medusa's severed head on her aegis or breastplate and on Zeus's shield. Other *gorgoneia* (images of Medusa's head) were installed on temples and other places to benefit from her protection, even after death. Ironically, *gorgoneia* were placed on heroes' shields, armor, and chariots to protect the Greek warriors engaged in destroying all threats to the new social order, including her own.

The fascination with Medusa did not diminish at the end of the Greek Classical Era. She continued to function as a lightning rod for prevailing cultural attitudes. During the Greco-Roman period, images of Medusa were reproduced for wealthy patrons on mosaics and sculptural reliefs as mostly young and beautiful rather than disturbingly ferocious. Nevertheless, Christian zealots, who were rising in prominence, considered all pagan images abominations to be destroyed, especially of the Gorgon Medusa. During the Medieval period in Europe, Christian scholars considered the beheading of Medusa by Perseus to be an allegory of the virtuous son of god destroying the manifestation of evil, intrinsic to all women, that threatens men's souls.

Renaissance artists, inspired by Greek mythological themes, created frighteningly realistic portrayals of decapitated women with snakes for hair. The elegantly crafted sculpture by Benvenuto Cellini of a youthful Perseus holding Medusa's head aloft while he stands on her decapitated body was erected in the center of Florence in the mid-16th century. This popular theme was emblematic of the Inquisitional murders of women taking place in many areas of Europe during that time, considered necessary to protect civil society from the dangers of uncontrolled female powers.[6] Later, during the 18th-19th centuries, Romantic artists, poets, and Decadents recast Medusa as a beautiful victim, not a monster. In their view, She represented the ecstatic discord between pain and pleasure, beauty and horror, and divinely forbidden sexuality.

But as the 20th century dawned, Freudian psychology promoted the regressive notion that women suffer an intrinsic deficiency resulting in "penis envy." Freud wrote that the "depreciation of women, horror of women, and a disposition to homosexuality are derived from the final conviction that women have no penis."[7] In his view, Medusa's face represents a "vagina dentata"—a hideous toothed vagina—surrounded by the writhing phalluses of castrated men.[8]

---

[6] Most of the tortures, beheadings, and burning of women in Italy took place in the North. The centers of Renaissance humanism in the city-states to the south had a controlling effect on the most extreme expressions of Inquisitional mania.
[7] Freud, Sigmund. "The Infantile Genital Organization," in *The Medusa Reader*, M. Garber and Nancy J. Vickers, eds. New York: Routledge, 2003, 85-86.
[8] Freud, Sigmund. "Medusa's Head" (1922), in *The Complete Psychological Works of Sigmund Freud,* vol. 15 (1921-22). London: Hogarth Press and the Institute of Psycho-Analysis.

Significant strides have been made by women throughout the world to challenge the deeply embedded misogyny that has plagued the lives of women and girls for millennia. Advancements (which are far from universal) such as the right to vote, to own property, to obtain a divorce, to control our own reproduction, and many other human rights have been achieved by women with great sacrifice and struggle. Nevertheless, the threat of censure, internalized as a template of fear and self-loathing, continues to enforce the physical and psychological silencing of women and girls, even in privileged cultural contexts.

The Gorgon Medusa presents herself to us here and now, requiring us to be fully present, to listen deeply—past the noise of accumulated judgments—to the Ancient Wisdom that is our true inheritance. As the Great Awakener, She reminds us of our mortality and encourages us to reclaim whatever has been silenced or diminished within us while we are privileged to be alive. We are admonished to have the courage to act and speak what is true, to trust ourselves to hold her gaze and know we will not be turned to stone.

A Note About Medusa's Language
Trista Hendren

Re-visioning Medusa contains a variety of writing styles from women around the world. Various forms of English are included in this anthology and we chose to keep spellings of the writers' place of origin to honor (or honour) each woman's unique voice.

It was the expressed intent of the editors to not police standards of citation, transliteration and formatting. Contributors have determined which citation style, italicization policy and transliteration system to adopt in their pieces. The resulting diversity is a reflection of the diversity of academic fields, genres and personal expressions represented by the authors.[9]

The thing I have specifically enjoyed about this anthology is that there is no "right" or "wrong" answer in our re-visioning of Medusa. Gerda Lerner's words hung in my head—and my heart—as a deep challenge throughout the creation of this anthology.

> "To step outside of patriarchal thought means... overcoming the deep-seated resistance within ourselves toward accepting ourselves and our knowledge as valid. It means getting rid of the great men in our heads and substituting for them ourselves, our sisters, our anonymous foremothers."[10]

I believe it is critically important to reclaim Medusa as our own. Many of the words contained in this anthology did not come easily to the authors. Facing Medusa head-on takes courage—She

---

[9] This paragraph is borrowed and adapted with love from *A Jihad for Justice: Honoring the Work and Life of Amina Wadud*. Edited by Kecia Ali, Juliane Hammer and Laury Silvers.

[10] Lerner, Gerda. *The Creation of Patriarchy*. Oxford University Press, 1987.

challenges and transforms us in ways that few other Goddesses do.

As Hélène Cixous wrote:

> "She alone dares and wishes to know from within, where she, the outcast, has never ceased to hear the resonance of fore-language. She lets the other language speak—the language of 1,000 tongues which knows neither enclosure nor death. To life she refuses nothing. Her language does not contain, it carries; it does not hold back, it makes possible."[11]

Love and blessings to you as you read the pages that follow.

---

[11] Cixous, Hélène. "The Laugh of the Medusa," translated by Paula and Keith Cohen. 1976.

Mother Medusa: Regenerative One
Glenys Livingstone, Ph.D.

I FIRST SAW HER IN MYSELF, and gave voice to Her, after presenting a paper on Women and Religion at the Women and Labour Conference in Australia in 1980; and the paper had attracted quite a bit of media attention. I felt myself to be seen as She was: that is, as some-thing completely out *in* and *of*, the wilderness— though I did not yet correctly name Her: I did not really know who She was at that time. I did not know my heritage then—my Hera-tage: it was only just beginning to emerge from the Great Below. As a method of processing this experience I had a dialogue with Society as an entity. It proceeded thus:

Society: *What is this thing that you are—where do you come from? Who dug you up? You are ghastly. You have snakes on your head for hair. You have demons within you. You are Lilith. You are damnation. Give me a chance and I will be rid of you—the likes of you I had hoped were burnt long ago. But you have crawled forth from the earth again. You have come like a poisonous gas: you will corrupt me and all that I feed on. I wish to exorcise your presence.*

Glenys: *You are right that I mean to be part of radically changing you. You flatter me to say that I am Lilith. You honour me to connect me with my sisters long gone. Am I so totally opposed to you? Have I grasped so clearly your demons—your shadow? Has some special darkness of yours come to rest so completely in me? When you see me you cringe so... as if I were a leper—unclean. Am I such a puzzle to you? Do I show so much of your inadequacy?*

Society: *You are like the one from whose mouth fell toads and frogs. How is it that I honour you with these things? Was Eve honourable?*

Glenys: *What of Joan of Arc? Your brothers called her witch and burnt her—then they canonized her later when they forgot her potency.*

And a little later I added: *You wish that I didn't exist, so in some ways you rob me of my existence. You will, not to give me a mirror by which I may see myself… though you do in a distorted fashion.*

At around the same time in my life I had been reading Robin Morgan's book of poems, *Monster*, and in particular, the poem by that name at the end of the book, in which she feels identified in mind, spirit and body—so completely—as monster, by the cultural context and even by her toddler son. She concludes:

> *May my hives bloom bravely until my flesh is aflame*
> *And burns through the cobwebs.*
> *May we go mad together, my sisters.*
> *May our labor agony in bringing forth this revolution*
> *be the death of all pain.*
>
> *May I learn how to survive until my part is finished.*
> *May I realize that I*
>   *am a*
> *monster. I am*
>   *a monster.*
> *I am a monster.*
> *And I am proud.*[12]

I did feel myself to be this monster. However I wasn't sure that I could bear it: my inner resources were meager, and I didn't really know how I could be proud. I had a dream at that time after presenting the conference paper, wherein I was an ancient woman

---

[12] Robin Morgan, *Monster,* p. 85-86. Lines from "Monster" excerpted with permission of the poet; Copyright 1970 by Robin Morgan; first published as the title poem in her book of poems *Monster* (Random House, 1970) and collected in her *Upstairs in the Garden: New and Selected Poems* (Norton, 1990).

on the plains dressed in animal skin and holding a spear. Words were spoken to me, telling me to rise up and that my ancient spear would find its mark; there was also notice of future wounding in the process. I felt strengthened in my wild mission to find Her and more words for Her—my wild mission to know Her more deeply.

So off I went to study, across the seas, alone—without family. Amongst the readings in the research process was Barbara Walker's *Woman's Encyclopedia of Myths and Secrets*: including in it an introduction to Medusa, in which Barbara Walker confirmed that despite patriarchal perceptions, Medusa may represent "an ancient, widely recognized symbol of divine female wisdom."[13] She was named at last, and fuller notice of Her character given. Then there was Hélène Cixous' ovarian work, *The Laugh of the Medusa*, which praised Medusa's wild beauty, and inspired further action and writing to restore this divine beauty. Hélène Cixous wrote: "Let the priests tremble, we're going to show them our sexts!"[14] I was beginning to grasp some threads. My journey with Her was just beginning, though I had no idea: life got busy and it would be another ten years before I really felt Her again, in devastating circumstance as is often Her way.

I was, after all, a daughter of the patriarchy, and real change in my core being was required: I felt strongly the cultural assignment as sex object, with no sense of organic agency—a colonized bodymind, vulnerable to predation. I was blessed however: my life fell apart. I wrote a little later in reflection:

> *What did it take… to develop a shell, a protective boundary, to pull the shades on the imposing mostly male Gaze, to allow a fertile darkness within my being, where "I" could begin? What did it take to create this kind of darkness, a safe place to Be, to shut out the world and scream "I"?... A sex*

---

[13] Barbara Walker, *The Woman's Encyclopaedia of Myths and Secrets*, p. 629.
[14] Hélène Cixous, *The Laugh of the Medusa*, p. 885.

> *object has to completely fall apart before she can rebuild herself in her own image. She has to fall into the mud, begin again, perform her own acts of Creation, mold herself of this solid material. It is out of the mud that the lotus blossoms. It does not grow on some pedestal, under the light of the eternal Gaze. How ironic that our paternal mythmakers made Medusa's gaze the deadly one!*[15]

In the process of rebuilding myself and my life, I began at last to facilitate classes, gathering groups of women for *Re-storying Goddess* as the classes were named... and so we did this in-forming for each other, filling our bodyminds with noble ancient images and story, and hearing each other into speech.[16] In these many classes and workshops I would always invoke the Crone aspect in this way:

> *There is a time for the waxing and there is a time for the waning. Medusa, Hecate, Kali... we call you. Once you were not separate, we restore you to your place in the cycle, in the communion.*

Gradually I was able to form the question in my mind, and later wrote it into my doctoral thesis[17] and then into my book:

> *What might be the consequences of changing our minds sufficiently, so that Medusa for instance, can be comprehended as metaphor for Divine Wisdom? Many scholars contend She once was understood this way. What might it mean for our minds to welcome Her back? Would*

---

[15] Glenys Livingstone, *PaGaian Cosmology*, p.75.
[16] Nelle Morton used this expression somewhere: "hearing each other into speech."
[17] Glenys Livingstone. *The Female Metaphor – Virgin, Mother, Crone – of the Dynamic Cosmological Unfolding: Her Embodiment in Seasonal Ritual as Catalyst for Personal and Cultural Change.*

that alter the way we relate to Earth, to Being?[18]

I was able at this time to identify Goddess—"the Female Metaphor" as I named Her, in all Her three qualities, with Cosmogenesis, the Western scientific story of the creative unfolding of the Cosmos, as told by Brian Swimme and Thomas Berry.[19] They describe these three qualities of Cosmogenesis as "the governing themes and the basal intentionality of all existence," characterizing the evolution of the universe "throughout time and space and at every level of reality."[20] And so, did I identify Goddess' three qualities: as primordial and all pervasive Creative Cosmic Dynamic. I now saw clearly Her aspect of Crone, Dark One, as essentially creative: the breaking down of the old, the "waning," was actually creative, in the context of the whole and larger picture, the communion.[21] With Her process, She allows space for renewal: I named Her as *She Who Creates the Space to Be*.

When I began the practice of celebrating the full year of seasonal ceremony in a serious committed manner in 1998—having noticed the power of such religious practice, the power of speaking with the Mother Cosmos in this way—I always wore a significant headpiece that actually was characteristic of the ancient primordial Medusa, though I did not know it. The artist who created the headpiece had named Her Melusine and that meant very little to me at the time also. The reason I bought the headpiece was because a child—"Stephanie" was her name—saw me trying it on and exclaimed "Fairy!" with delight: I was seduced. I had no idea who She was, and only began to play with the headpiece and the armband that came with it, in the *Re-storying Goddess* workshops a few years after buying it: indeed, all the women played with Her. But with the serious engagement in the ceremonial celebration of

---

[18] Glenys Livingstone, *PaGaian Cosmology*, p. 66.
[19] Brian Swimme and Thomas Berry, *The Universe Story*, pp. 71-79.
[20] Brian Swimme and Thomas Berry, *The Universe Story*, p.71.
[21] I develop this further in *PaGaian Cosmology*, pp. 117-120 in particular.

the full year of the Seasonal Moments I decorated Her—this headpiece—each time according to the themes of the Season and wore Her. This headpiece became an entity over the years; I wrote:

> *As I pace the circle... I see "Her" as She has been through the Seasons... the black and gold of Samhain, the deep red, white and evergreen of Winter, the white and blue of Imbolc, the flowers of Eostar, the rainbow ribbons of Beltane, the roses of Summer, the seed pods and wheat of Lammas, and now the Autumn leaves. I see in my mind's eye, and feel, Her changes. I am learning... The Mother knowledge grows within me.*[22]

Only gradually have I come to identify Her snake coils and bird wings, as an ancient combination representative of Medusa as Miriam Robbins Dexter describes in this anthology.[23] I realize now that I had been invoking Medusa; calling Her into my being, embodying Her in Seasonal ceremony, embedding Her regenerative creativity in my life. As Marija Gimbutas points out, the earliest Greek gorgons as Medusa was, or wherever Goddess appeared as a mask of death, She was never separate from symbols of regeneration.[24]

I did not "choose" Her. She chose me it seems. I was a space wherein She could grow, and She was re-storing the integrity and nobility of my femaleness: perhaps "the curse" in all its valences of body cycle, spirit and mind that I held in my female being and story, was actually a portal of deep connection to Earth as Mother. My cultural context has tried to ignore this Beauty and ubiquitously abuses it. Was the shame and the horror actually a blessing? Was She—the Medusa and all She represented actually beautiful, as Hélène Cixous and others had perceived? Perhaps this was why

---

[22] Glenys Livingstone, *PaGaian Cosmology,* p. 181.
[23] Miriam Robbins Dexter, p. 11.
[24] Marija Gimbutas, *The Language of the Goddess*, p. xxiii and p.207.

they couldn't bear to look at Her? I began to understand that Her awesome visage was indeed characteristic of any ultimate Deity: fearsome to behold, but it included intense beauty as well as terror.

Still, She dawns in me, gradually rising and coming to fullness, the Regenerative One whom She is. Still, I learn how the darkness and the shedding of the old, which She represents, is simultaneously space for renewal—one does not happen without the other, whether or not one can see it. Gradually Her ancient knowledge of never-ending renewal is restoring to my being.

© Glenys Livingstone 2017 C.E.

REFERENCES:

Cixous, Hélène. "The Laugh of the Medusa" (trans. Keith Cohen and Paula Cohen). Signs 1 no. 22, Summer 1976, p.875-893.

Gimbutas, Marija. *The Language of the Goddess*. NY: HarperCollins, 1991.

Livingstone, Glenys. *PaGaian Cosmology: Re-inventing Earth-based Goddess Religion.* NE: iUniverse, 2005.

Livingstone, Glenys. *The Female Metaphor – Virgin, Mother, Crone – of the Dynamic Cosmological Unfolding: Her Embodiment in Seasonal Ritual as Catalyst for Personal and Cultural Change*. Ph.D. thesis, University of Western Sydney, 2002.

Morgan, Robin. *Monster*. NY: Vintage Books. 1972.

Swimme, Brian and Berry, Thomas. *The Universe Story.* New York: HarperCollins, 1992.

Walker, Barbara. *The Woman's Encyclopaedia of Myths and Secrets*. San Francisco: Harper and Row, 1983.

Ceremonial Headpiece Invoking Ancient Medusa
Glenys Livingstone, Ph.D.

Yew Medusa
Cristina Biaggi, Ph.D.

Self-Portrait, 1980.

Medusa: Ferocious and Beautiful, Petrifying and Healing: Through the Words of the Ancients[25]

Miriam Robbins Dexter, Ph.D.

Introduction

This article looks at the Greco-Roman Gorgon, Medusa, cross-culturally, through texts and iconography, in order to examine her origins as well as her multifaceted functions. I will show that Medusa is a compilation of Neolithic European, Semitic, and Indo-European mythology and iconography. Iconographically, two very different depictions coalesce in the Classical-Age Medusa: the Neolithic Goddess of birth, death, and regeneration, who is represented as bird, snake, or bird-snake hybrid; and the Near Eastern demon Humbaba whose severed head is, like Medusa's, used in an apotropaic manner. Medusa is ferocious but, as we will see, she is a healer as well as a destroyer. Because she is often viewed as frightening in Indo-European cultures, this other side of her is often overlooked.

The Name of Medusa

Philologically, the name Medusa means the "ruling one."[26] But by the time of the earliest Greek texts which contain myth, those of Homer, Medusa was not a ruler but a monster, associated with the land of Hades. In the poetry of Hesiod, Medusa became the only mortal among three Gorgon sisters. The adjective *gorgos* (γοργός)

---

[25] This material was first presented at the conference, "Female Mysteries of the Substratum," held in Rila, Bulgaria, June 2-13, 2004. I am grateful to Joan Marler and my colleagues in the international Institute of Archaeomythology for their suggestions. The material was later published, in somewhat different form from this paper, in the *Journal of Feminist Studies in Religion*. (*JFSR* 26.1 (2010) 25–41). I also thank the UCLA Center for the Study of Women for their support.

[26] This is the present participle of the Greek verb μέδω, "I rule." Medusa, or Medousa, is spelled with a short -e- in Greek, as opposed to the long ē found in Mēdea.

means "terrible," "fierce," and "frightful." That is, she was considered to be monstrous. However, as we will learn from the Classical texts, it is important to see all facets of what male-centered cultures have labeled a "feminine monster." Medusa was viewed very ambivalently, and she was very deeply faceted.

Modern Western culture has tended to dwell too much on the character of her "anger." For example, a misogynist trend in psychoanalysis focuses upon her paralyzing qualities, viewing her as a deflator of masculine strength, while curiously, at other times, seeing her snaky persona as phallic. Radical feminists also often dwell upon her anger, identifying it with a fiercely liberating women's rage. That surely helps many women, but it doesn't effectively disrupt the misogyny involved in labeling a female figure as "monstrous." Thus, a historical and cross-cultural exploration of Medusa can contribute to a feminist effort to honor and articulate the complexity of the divine female.

Texts and Myths

In order to discover Medusa's earliest textual meanings and symbols, and to understand the development of her character and iconography, I decided to translate her myths from the Greek and Latin texts, in chronological order. My translations are quite literal, so that the meanings of the texts can be as clear as possible. I begin with the earliest Greek literary texts, Homer's *Iliad* and *Odyssey*.

In the *Iliad*, dating to approximately 750 BCE, Medusa is not named, but one finds here the first reference to a Gorgon. In this text, Athena puts on her aegis, on which are depicted, among others, Fear (Phobos), Strife (Eris), and "the Gorgon head of the terrible monster, terrible and fearful, a portent of aegis-holding Zeus."[27]

---

[27] Homer, *Iliad* 5.741-742. Ca. 750 BCE:
ἐν δέ τε Γοργείη κεφαλὴ δεινοῖ πελώρου, δεινή τε σμερδνή τε, Διὸς τέρας αἰγιόχοιο
The text may be found in *Homeri Opera*. Thomas W. Allen, ed. 1961. (Oxford: Clarendon Press). Unless otherwise indicated, all translations in this article are

There are no references to wings or snakes in Homer, but, just as on Athena's aegis, the Gorgon is paired with snakes on the shield of Agamemnon:

> "And on it was put as a crown the Gorgon, with ferocious face [or: bushy-faced[28]], with dreadful glance, and about her were Terror and Flight. A shield-strap of silver was attached to it, and there also was coiled upon it a dark blue snake..."[29]

In fact, examples of shields with Gorgon heads abound in Greek iconography.[30] This may be a natural psychological function, using a fearsome head in order to frighten off the enemy. The Maori warriors of New Zealand make Medusa-like faces when they go into battle. Elsewhere in the *Iliad*, Homer describes the Trojan hero Hector's eyes, using the Gorgon as metaphor: "Having Gorgon eyes or those of man-destroying Ares." (Homer, *Iliad* 8.349). Thus, her staring eyes play a role in her myth from her textual inception; Medusa's eye petrifies.[31] Her "evil" eye brings death.

Although the disembodied head of the Gorgon must have been depicted or mythologized by 750 BCE, it is likely that the story of Medusa and Perseus was not known. There is no reference in the *Iliad* to Medusa's decapitation by Perseus, even though Perseus is

---

by the author. Dating for all Classical authors follows the *Oxford Classical Dictionary*, Third Edition. (Oxford: University Press, 1996, 2000).

[28] The Greek word is βλοσυρῶπις (*blosurōpis*). See Georg Autenrieth, ed., *A Homeric Dictionary*. Transl. Robert P. Keep. (New York: Harper and Brothers, 1876 [1966]), 61.

[29] Homer, *Iliad*, 11.36-37:
τῇ δ' ἐπὶ μὲν Γοργὼ βλοσυρῶπις ἐστεφάνωτο δεινὸν δερκομένη, περὶ δὲ Δεῖμός τε Φόβος τε.
τῆς δ' ἐξ ἀργύρεος τελαμὼν ἦν· αὐτὰρ ἐπ' αὐτοῦ κυάνεος ἐλέλικτο δράκων...

[30] For a discussion of the Gorgon head depicted on shields throughout several centuries of Greek art, with cross-cultural comparisons, see Stephen R. Wilk, *Medousa: Solving the Mystery of the Gorgon* (Oxford: University Press, 2000), 145-160.

[31] Cf. the French *méduser*, "to petrify."

mentioned twice.[32] Here, he already has mythology—he is son of Danaë, and he is an outstanding warrior. In Book 19, he even has a son of his own. But his name is not linked here with Medusa's. In the *Odyssey* (ca. 725 BCE) as well, the Gorgon is not yet connected with Perseus. She is a fearsome creature who dwells in the Underworld. As Odysseus says,

> "...pale [lit. 'yellow-green'] dread seized me, lest illustrious Persephone might send forth upon me, from the house of Hades, the head of the Gorgon, the terrible monster."[33]

By approximately 700 BCE, we do find Medusa and Perseus connected in myth, in the *Theogony* of the poet Hesiod, who gives a catalogue of the genealogies of the Goddesses and Gods:

> "And again, Ceto bore to Phorcys the fair-cheeked Graiae, sisters gray-haired from birth, whom indeed both the deathless gods and men who walk on earth call the Graiae, beautifully-robed Pemphredo, and saffron-robed Enyo, and the Gorgons who dwell on the other side of glorious Ocean in the most remote land, towards Night, where [live] the clear-voiced Hesperides, Sthenno, and Euryale, and Medusa, suffering miseries: she was mortal, but the two [sisters] were immortal and ageless. With this woman [that is, Medusa] lay the dark-blue-haired[34] one [Poseidon] in a soft meadow [35] in the midst of spring flowers. Now, when

---

[32] Homer, *Iliad* 14.320, 19.123.
[33] Homer, *Odyssey* 11.633-35:
ἐμὲ δὲ χλωρὸν δέος ᾕρει, μή μοι Γοργείην κεφαλὴν δεινοῖο πελώρου ἐξ Ἀίδεω πέμψειεν ἀγαυὴ Περσεφόνεια.
[34] Hesiod, as well as Homer, used the Greek epithet Κυανοχαίτης (Kuanochaites) to mean 'dark blue- maned,' as of a horse. See Henry G. Liddell and Robert Scott, *Greek-English Lexicon*, 9th edition (New York: Harper and Brothers 1856 [1961]): 1004. Since Poseidon was known to have taken the shape of a stallion—for example, when he raped Demeter—this is an apt term for him.
[35] Greek ἐν μαλακῷ λειμῶνι (en malako leimoni). This was also a term used for a woman's genital area. See Liddell and Scott (1856 [1961]: 1035).

Perseus cut off her head, both great Chrysaor and the horse, Pegasus, leapt forth."[36]

Even early on in the texts, Medusa is attractive enough for the god Poseidon to want to sleep with her. In fact, it is possible that Medusa was never portrayed as uniformly grotesque. She was portrayed early on in both text and iconography as a beautiful young woman.[37] Although Medusa is not yet snaky-haired in the *Theogony*, in the Shield of Herakles, which was attributed to Hesiod,[38] Perseus decapitates Medusa and flees, chased by Medusa's Gorgon sisters:

---

[36] Hesiod, *Theogony* 270-81:
Φόρκυϊ δ' αὖ Κητὼ Γραίας τέκε καλλιπαρήους ἐκ γενετῆς πολιάς, τὰς δὴ Γραίας καλέουσιν ἀθάνατοί τε θεοὶ χαμαὶ ἐρχόμενοί τ' ἄνθρωποί, Πεμφρηδώ τ' εὔπεπλον Ἐνυώ τε κροκόπεπλον, Γοργούς θ', αἳ ναίουσι πέρην κλυτοῦ Ὠκεανοῖο ἐσχατιῇ πρὸς Νυκτός, ἵν' Ἑσπερίδες λιγύφωνοι, Σθεννώ τ' Εὐρυάλη τε Μέδουσά τε λυγρὰ παθοῦσα. ἣ μὲν ἔην θνητή, αἳ δ' ἀθάνατοι καὶ ἀγήρῳ, αἱ δύο· τῇ δὲ μιῇ παρελέξατο Κυανοχαίτης ἐν μαλακῷ λειμῶνι καὶ ἄνθεσιν εἰαρινοῖσιν. τῆς δ' ὅτε δὴ Περσεὺς κεφαλὴν ἀπεδειροτόμησεν, ἔκθορε Χρυσάωρ τε μέγας καὶ Πήγασος ἵππος.
The text for the citations from Heriod is in *Hesiod, Opera*, Friedrich Solmsen, ed. 1970. (Oxford: Clarendon Press).

[37] Daniel E. Gershonson, in "The Beautiful Gorgon and Indo-European Parallels," *The Mankind Quarterly* 29 (4) (1989): 373-90, demonstrates that throughout Greco-Roman texts, Medusa was portrayed as beautiful as well as ugly. Gershonson cites Hesiod, *Theogony* 278-279 and Ovid, *Metamorphoses* 4.794-861, and I would add the *Odes* of Pindar (see below). According to Gershonson, "the beautiful face of the Gorgon, which is extremely ancient in Greek literature, cannot be the 'logical end' of an intellectual development. Rather it is very likely to be an ever-actualisable alternate expression of the Gorgoneion, with its own meaning vis-à-vis the horrifying monstrous Gorgon's head" (377). In fact, I believe that the Gorgon is the same as the ugly old woman who is a shape-changer in Old Irish myth. In Old Irish, she is the Goddess Sovereignty—Flaith—who is alternatively a beautiful young woman and an ugly crone. See Miriam Robbins Dexter and Starr Goode, "The Sheela na gigs, Sexuality, and the Goddess in Ancient Ireland," *Irish Journal of Feminist Studies* 4 (2) (2002): 65.

[38] This traditional attribution of the Shield of Herakles to Hesiod has been challenged. See Marjorie Garber and Nancy J. Vickers, 2003, Th*e Medusa Reader*. New York: Routledge: 11.

"And after him the Gorgons went, monstrous and unspeakable... and from their girdles two serpents hung down, their heads arched."[39]

By the time of the Greek poet Pindar, ca. 500 BCE, serpents were firmly affixed to the Gorgons' heads, in myth as well as in art.[40] Pindar worked rich mythological texts into his odes celebrating victories at the Olympian, Pythian, Nemean, and Isthmian Games. He says:

"Pallas Athena invented the baleful funeral song of the bold Gorgons, weaving it together. This [song], poured forth with direful toil, Perseus heard, from beneath the terrible serpent-heads [of] the maidens, when he destroyed the third sister."[41]

Indeed, the sight of the Medusa-head will turn people—men and women, and, as later texts tell us, even animals—to stone:

"[The son of Danaë] slew the Gorgon, and he returned bearing her head, dappled with the locks of serpents, [and bearing] a stony death for the islanders [the people of

---

[39] Hesiod, *Shield of Herakles* 229-235. Ca. 700-500 BCE:
ταὶ δὲ μετ' αὐτὸν   Γοργόνες ἄπλητοί τε καὶ οὐ φαταὶ ἐρρώοντο   ἰέμεναι μαπέειν...   ...ἐπὶ δὲ ζώνῃσι δράκοντε   δοιὼ ἀπῃωρεῦντ' ἐπικυρτώοντε κάρηνα   λίχμαζον δ' ἄρα τώ γε...

[40] Vicki Noble (personal communication June, 2004) reminds me that Medusa's snakes indicate that she is mesmerizing through her power, just as snakes can mesmerize. Further, she says, in the West, woman is split off from this locus of power.

[41] Pindar, *Pythia* 12.7-12:
Παλλὰς ἐφεῦρε θρασειᾶν Γοργόνων   οὔλιον θρῆνον διαπλέξαισ' Ἀθάνα·   τὸν παρθενίοις ὑπό τ' ἀπλάτοις ὀφίων κεφαλαῖς   ἄϊε λειβόμενον δυσπενθέϊ σὺν καμάτῳ,   Περσεὺς ὁπότε τρίτον ἄνυσσεν κασιγνητᾶν μέρος.

Texts by Pindar are in *Pindar, Carmina cum Fragmenta*, C.M. Bowra, ed. 1935-58. Oxford: Clarendon Press. Pindar's dates are 518 - ca. 438 BCE.

Seriphus]."[42]

Medusa is terrifying and deadly; but she is beautiful as well as frightening when Pindar describes how:

> "...the head of the beautiful-cheeked Medusa was carried off by the son of Danaë, who, we assert, came into being because of a shower of gold."[43]

Pindar also tells us of Medusa's offspring, Pegasus. Here too Medusa is closely connected with snakes:

> "Pegasus, the son of the snaky Gorgon..."[44]

The Greek historian, Herodotus, (ca. 560-420 BCE) connects Perseus and the Gorgon, and places them in Libya:

> "[The people of Chemmis in Egypt] told too how [Perseus] came to Egypt for the reason which the Greeks recount— [that is,] to bring the head of the Gorgon from Libya..."[45]

---

[42] Pindar, *Pythia* 10.46-48:
ἔπεφνέν τε Γοργόνα, καὶ ποικίλον κάρα   δρακόντων φόβαισιν ἤλυθε νασιώταις   λίθινον θάνατον φέρων.

[43] Pindar, *Pythia* 12.16-18:
εὐπαράου κρᾶτα συλάσαις Μεδοίσας   υἱὸς Δανάας· τὸν ἀπὸ χρυσοῦ φαμεν αὐτορύτου   ἔμμεναι.

[44] Pindar, *Olympia* 13.63-64:
ὃς τᾶς ὀφιώδεος υἱόν ποτε Γοργόνος ...   Πάγασον...
Pindar also alludes briefly to the myth of Medusa and Perseus in *Nemea* 10.4, and to the father of the Gorgons (Phorcys, who was also grandfather of the Cyclops, Polyphemos) in *Dithyramb* 1.5.

[45] Herodotus, *Histories* 2.91:
Περσέα... ἀπικόμενον δὲ αὐτὸν ἐς Αἴγυπτον κατ' αἰτίην τὴν καὶ Ἕλληνες λέγουσι, οἴσοντα ἐκ Λιβύης τὴν Γοργοῦς κεφαλήν, ἔφασαν ἐλθεῖν καὶ παρὰ σφέας
The text is in *Herodotus, Histories*. Carl Hude, ed. 1908. Oxford: Clarendon Press.

In the Classical era in which the Greek tragedian Euripides (ca. 480-407/6 BCE) wrote his plays, Gorgon-antefixes were affixed to walls. These Gorgon heads were apotropaic: they would have protected the temple and other buildings in the city. In one of Euripides' plays, Ion, priest of Phoebus Apollo, tells us that on the walls of the temple, "The Gorgons are all around."[46]

Here too, Medusa is associated with serpents. In this play, Creusa, the Queen of Athens, describes an embroidered robe: "A Gorgon in the middle threads of a robe... it is bordered with serpents in the manner of an aegis."[47]

In addition to the Gorgon head as protectress, we learn something important in the *Ion* about the function of Medusa's blood, and about her larger function as well. Queen Creusa tells an old servant about Medusa's blood, which Athena gave to Erichthonius, the ancestor of the Athenian line:

> "Two drops of blood from the Gorgon... One [is] deadly; the other brings healing of diseases."[48]

Thus, there is an ambivalence here about the death-aspect of the Goddess. Clearly, she represents regeneration as well as death. Indeed, the venom of a snake can be both poison and antitoxin.[49] As I will discuss on the pages that follow, Medusa holds

---

[46] Euripides, *Ion* 224:
ἀμφὶ δὲ γοργόνες.
The text for the sources from Euripides is in *Euripides, Fabulae* II. Gilbert Murray, ed. 1902. Reprint 1951. (Oxford: Clarendon Press).

[47] Euripides, *Ion* 1421-23:
Γοργὼν μὲν ἐν μέσοισιν ἠτρίοις πέπλων...κεκρασπέδωται δ' ὄφεσιν αἰγίδος τρόπον.

[48] Euripides, *Ion* 1003-1005:
δισσοὺς σταλαγμοὺς αἵματος Γοργοῦς ἄπο...τὸν μὲν θανάσιμον, τὸν δ' ἀκεσφόρον νόσων.

[49] The Buddhist Goddess Jāgulī is also related to snakes, and she has poisonous qualities. These qualities are shamanistic, because, just as Medusa's, the liquid

here the functions of the prehistoric Goddess of the life continuum: birth, death, and then regeneration. She is multifunctional and multidimensional and she should be viewed in all of her complexity, through a non-patriarchal lens.

In the second century BCE, Apollodorus shows an expansion of this dual aspect of Medusa's blood:

> "[They say that] Asclepius... having received from Athena blood flowing from the veins of the Gorgon, used that flowing from the left side for the destruction of humanity, [while] he used that from the right side for saving [humanity], and because of this, that he roused the dead."[50]

Apollodorus gives a very patriarchal reason for Athena's animosity—female competition and vanity on the part of Athena:

> "It is said by some that Medusa was beheaded because of Athena; they say that, in fact, the Gorgon wished to compare herself to her [Athena] in [regard to] beauty."[51]

---

she pours from her pitcher is manifested both as healing nectar and poison. See Miranda Shaw, *Buddhist Goddesses of India* (Princeton, N.J./Oxford: Princeton University Press, 2006), 227.

[50] Apollodorus, *Atheniensis Bibliothecae* (The Library) 3.10.3:
Ἀσκληπιὸν…παρὰ γὰρ Ἀθηνᾶς λαβὼν τὸ ἐκ τῶν φλεβῶν τῆς Γοργόνος ῥυὲν αἷμα, τῷ μὲν ἐκ τῶν ἀριστερῶν ῥυέντι πρὸς φθορὰν ἀνθρώπων ἐχρῆτο, τῷ δὲ ἐκ τῶν δεξιῶν πρὸς σωτηρίαν, καὶ διὰ τούτου τοὺς τεθνηκότας ἀνήγειρεν.

The text is in *Apollodorus, The Library* I. E. Clavier, ed. 1805. (Paris: Delance et Lesueur.) This particular passage may be from the later Pseudo-Apollodorus. Some scholars now believe that the works attributed to Apollodorus were actually composed up to a few hundred years after his lifetime. See Marjorie Garber and Nancy J. Vickers, eds., *The Medusa Reader* (New York: Routledge, 2003), 23.

[51] Apollodorus, *Atheniensis Bibliothecae* 2.4.3:
λέγεται δὲ ὑπ' ἐνίων ὅτι δι' Ἀθηνᾶν ἡ Μέδουσα ἐκαρατομήθη·
φασὶ δὲ ὅτι καὶ περὶ κάλλους ἠθέλησεν ἡ Γοργὼ αὐτῇ συγκριθῆναι.

Apollodorus also gives a more expansive iconography of the Gorgons:

> "The Gorgons had heads twined around with the horny scales of serpents, and huge teeth [i.e., tusks] like [those of] boars, and bronze hands, and golden wings, by means of which they flew. And they turned to stone those who looked upon them."[52]

Here, the Gorgons are bird/snakes, similar to Neolithic European and Near Eastern female figures.

Perhaps evoking the etymology of Medusa as "the ruling one," Diodorus Siculus, in the mid-first century BCE, describes the Gorgons as Amazon queens ruling in the area of Lake Tritonis in North Africa, in Greek called Libya:

> "But the Gorgons, having increased in power in later times, were utterly subdued again by Perseus, the son of Zeus, at the very time when Medusa ruled them; and at last both they [i.e., the Gorgons] and the race of the Amazons were wholly destroyed by Heracles, when, invading lands to the west, he set up dedicatory stones in Libya, thinking that it would be terrible if, choosing to do good deeds for the general race of humanity, he should allow any of the nations to be ruled by women."[53]

---

[52] Apollodorus, *Atheniensis Bibliothecae* 2.4.2:
εἶχον δὲ αἱ Γοργόνες κεφαλὰς μὲν περιεσπειραμένας φολίσι δρακόντων, ὀδόντας δὲ μεγάλους ὡς συῶν, καὶ χεῖρας χαλκᾶς, καὶ πτέρυγας χρυσᾶς, δι' ὧν ἐπέτοντο. τοὺς δὲ ἰδόντας λίθους ἐποίουν.

Thus, anyone—not just a man—who looks at a Gorgon's face will turn to stone.

[53] Diodorus Siculus, *Bibliothēkē* 3.55.3:
...τὰς δὲ Γοργόνας ἐν τοῖς ὕστερον χρόνοις αὐξηθείσας πάλιν ὑπὸ Περσέως τοῦ Διὸς καταπολεμηθῆναι, καθ' ὃν καιρὸν ἐβασίλευεν αὐτῶν Μέδουσα· τὸ δὲ τελευταῖον ὑφ' Ἡρακλέους ἄρδην ἀναιρεθῆναι ταύτας τε καὶ τὸ τῶν Ἀμαζόνων ἔθνος, καθ' ὃν καιρὸν τοὺς πρὸς ἑσπέραν τόπους ἐπελθὼν ἔθετο τὰς ἐπὶ τῆς

Medusa was indeed understood as a ruler. However, according to Diodorus Siculus, Herakles, wanting to be a true hero, must save the world from female rule.

The Roman poet Ovid (43 BCE - 17 CE) also associates Medusa with Libya, and as the origin of the Libyan snakes:

> "And as the conqueror [Perseus] hung suspended over the Libyan sands, bloody drops fell from the Gorgon's head; the earth receiving them, turned them into manifold snakes. Whence that land is full of, and infested with, snakes."[54]

Ovid also presents the most familiar story of Perseus and Medusa to non-specialists. In the land of the Gorgons, the Gorgon-heads had turned all living creatures into stone, and Perseus is helped by Athena to avoid this fate:

> "[Perseus told how] he had reached the homes of the Gorgons, and that he saw far and wide, through the fields and along the roads, likenesses of people[55] and of animals, turned into stone once they saw Medusa's face. But [he said] that he himself had viewed the likeness of dreadful Medusa reflected in the bronze shield which his left hand bore, and while a heavy sleep held both the snakes and her, he had struck off her head from her neck, and from the blood of the

---

Λιβύης στήλας, δεινὸν ἡγούμενος, εἰ προελόμενος τὸ γένος κοινῇ τῶν ἀνθρώπων εὐεργετεῖν περιόψεταί τινα τῶν ἐθνῶν γυναικοκρατούμενα.
The text for Diodorus Siculus may be found in *Diodori Bibliotheca Historica*, Ludwig Dindorf, ed. 1866, Leipzig: Teubner.
[54] Ovid, *Metamorphoses* 4.617-620:
Cumque super Libycas victor penderet harenas, Gorgonei capitis guttae cecidere cruentae;
quas humus exceptas varios animavit in angues, unde frequens illa est infestaque terra colubris.
The texts for Ovid are in *Ovid, Works*. R. Merkel, ed. 1907. (Leipzig: Teubner).
[55] Ovid uses the Latin word, *hominum*, which refers to people: both women and men; he does not use the Latin *vir*, which refers to heroic men.

mother were born fleet-winged Pegasus and his brother."[56]

Thus, Perseus rather unheroically killed Medusa while she slept, using a mirror to allow himself to safely see Medusa's face and avoid the magic of her gaze. Indeed, the bronze mirror is historically the priestess/shaman's tool, rather than the tool of the young male hero.[57] A further clue to the shamanic potential of Medusa's story is that Medusa cannot be found without the help of the Graiai, three sisters who have one eye and one tooth between them. The one-eyed one sees deeply into the other worlds.

Ovid also gives us a glimpse of the violent transformation of the beautiful Medusa into the only Gorgon with snaky hair:

> "She was most beautiful in form, and the envied hope of many suitors. And there was no part of her more attractive than her hair: I learned that [from someone who] said that he had seen her. The ruler of the sea [Neptune] is said to

---

[56] Ovid, *Metamorphoses* 4.779-786:
Gorgoneas tetigisse domos passimque per agros perque vias vidisse hominum simulacra ferarumque
in silicem ex ipsis visa conversa Medusa. Se tamen horrendae clipei, quem laeva gerebat,
aere repercusso formam adspexisse Medusae, dumque gravis somnus colubrasque ipsamque tenebat,
eripuisse caput collo; pennisque fugacem Pegason et fratrem matris de sanguine natos.

[57] See V.M. Masson and V.I. Sarianidi, *Central Asia: Turkmenia before the Achaemenids* (London: Thames and Hudson, 1972), 122. Further, the prolific first-century CE writer Lucan tells us, "[Athena] told Perseus that, at the border of the Libyan land, he should turn towards the rising sun [lit. Phoebus (Apollo)], plowing with backwards flight the Gorgon's realm." (Lucan, *Pharsalia* 9.666-670:
...terraeque in fine Libyssae Persea Phoebeos converti iussit ad ortus, Gorgonos averso sulcantem regna volatu...
The text is in *M. Annaei Lucani Pharsalia*. C. E. Haskins, ed. 1887. London: G. Bell.)
That is, Medusa was to be killed at sunrise: Medusa, the shaman-priestess, was to be killed at a liminal time, a magical time, in keeping with Medusa's own magical power.

have raped her in the temple of Minerva. The daughter of Jupiter [that is, Minerva/Athena] turned away and hid her chaste face in her aegis; nor was this deed unpunished. She turned the hair of the Gorgon into ugly snakes."[58]

The patriarchal regime in which the rapist goes unpunished and the raped one is caused to suffer is obvious. We should recall that Hesiod gives another story of Poseidon (the Greek equivalent of the Roman Neptune) and Medusa; in the *Theogony*, they lay together in a pasture full of flowers—a much more life-affirming scene than a rape in the temple of Athena/Minerva. Later authors such as Ovid wanted to explain why Athena wears Medusa's head in her aegis and thus in his text Medusa directly offended Athena.

Two second-century Greek writers attest to the ongoing recognition of the complexity and power of Medusa. Lucian [59] echoes the tradition of Medusa's beauty in his view that it was the

---

[58] Ovid, *Metamorphoses* 4.794-801:
clarissima forma multorumque fuit spes invidiosa procorum illa, nec in tota conspectior ulla capillis
pars fuit: inveni, qui se vidisse referret. hanc pelagi rector templo vitiasse Minervae
dicitur: aversa est et castos aegide voltus nata Iovis texit, neve hoc inpune fuisset, Gorgoneum crinem turpes mutavit in hydros.
As do many Greco-Roman authors, Lucan discusses Medusa's snaky hair— but with a twist (Lucan, *Pharsalia* 9.632-53): "The snakes used to whip against Medusa's neck—to her delight—her hair unbound, hanging down her back, in feminine mode. The serpents, [heads] lifted up, stood up at her forehead [that is, forming bangs]. And when her hair was combed, the snaky venom flowed... No living being [could] stand the sight, and even the Gorgon's snakes used to avoid [her] face, slithering backwards [from her forehead]."
Femineo cui more comae per terga solutae, Ipsa flagellabant gaudentis colla Medusae.
Surgunt adversa subrectae fronte colubrae, vipereumque fluit de pexo crine venenum...
Nullum animal visus patiens, ipsique retrorsum effusi faciem vitabant Gorgonis angues.
[59] Lucian is to be distinguished from the Roman poet Lucan, cited above.

beauty of the Gorgons which paralyzed:

> "The Beauty of the Gorgons, inasmuch as it is most powerful and that it deals with [is in company with] the most vital aspects of the soul, forthwith drives the
> beholders senseless and makes them speechless, so that, as the myth indicates and people say, they were turned into stone, from astonishment."[60]

The Greek traveler Pausanias, writing approximately 150 CE, tells a euhemerizing story, in which Medusa is an African Amazon, ruling over those who lived near Lake Triton. Perseus makes war upon her: he cuts off her head and takes it to Greece. Subsequently, he was said to have buried Medusa's head in the *agora* in Argos, in order to protect the city:

> "Not far from the building in the market-place of the Argives there is a mound of earth. In it, they say, lies the head of the Gorgon, Medusa."[61]

Again, the head of Medusa is protective and apotropaic. Few people would want to bury the head of a purely malevolent being in a sacred precinct.

---

[60] Lucian, *The Hall* 19:
τὸ δὲ τῶν Γοργόνων κάλλος, ἅτε βιαιότατόν τε ὂν καὶ τοῖς καιριωτάτοις τῆς ψυχῆς ὁμιλοῦν, εὐθὺς ἐξίστη τοὺς ἰδόντας καὶ ἀφώνους ἐποίει, ὡς δὲ ὁ μῦθος βούλεται καὶ λέγεται, λίθινοι ἐγίγνοντο ὑπὸ θαύματος.

The text is in *Lucianus*. Carl Jacobitz, ed. 1966. Hildesheim: G. Olms. Ca. 120-180 CE.

[61] Pausanias, *Description of Greece*: 2.21.5-6:
τοῦ δὲ ἐν τῇ ἀγορᾷ τῶν Ἀργείων οἰκοδομήματος οὐ μακρὰν χῶμα γῆς ἐστιν· ἐν δὲ αὐτῷ κεῖσθαι τὴν Μεδούσης λέγουσι τῆς Γοργόνος κεφαλήν.

The text is in *Pausanias: Graeciae Descriptio* I-II. M.H. Rocha-Pereira, ed. 1973-77. Leipzig: Teubner.

These Greco-Roman authors believed that Medusa was beautiful and horrific, that her gaze turned people to stone but that her blood could heal; that she was multivalent and multifunctional.

Iconography

There are many theories about which mythical figures were antecedents to Medusa. It is likely that her tapestry weaves together threads which stretch back in time to European and Near Eastern Neolithic cultures, and which are reflected in the earliest Neolithic shamanic figures, and in the early historic demon- and death-figures throughout Europe, the Near East, and elsewhere in the ancient world. It is likely that the range of ways in which Medusa was viewed, from positive to negative, reflects the range of spheres of the Neolithic Goddesses of birth, death, and regeneration, and the negative stress given to death Goddesses by early historic Western writers who viewed death as an end of existence, rather than as part of a Great Round. In this section, I will discuss several possible threads in the tapestry of Medusa's multifaceted iconography.

The Neolithic Bird and Snake Goddesses

In the Neolithic period, throughout Europe and the Near East, there appear figurines which represent bird/women, snake/women, and bird/snake/woman hybrids.[62] Since Goddesses with bird and snake

---

[62] See the Cretan bird-faced female figure with a snake draped over her shoulders: Heraklion Museum, Crete; pre-1700 BCE. For an in-depth discussion of Neolithic European and Near Eastern bird and snake figures and their degeneration into early historic witches and monsters, see Miriam Robbins Dexter, "The Frightful Goddess: Birds, Snakes and Witches," in *Varia on the Indo-European Past: Papers in Memory of Marija Gimbutas,* ed. Miriam Robbins Dexter and Edgar C. Polomé. Journal of Indo-European Studies Monograph #19 (Washington, DC: The Institute for the Study of Man, 1997), 124-154. For updated versions with many images see "The Monstrous Goddess: The Degeneration of Ancient Bird and Snake Goddesses into Historic Age Witches and Monsters." *Izkustvo & Ideologiya: Ivan Marazov Decet Godini Po-K'sno (Art and Ideology: Festschrift for Ivan Marazov).* The anthology is in Bulgarian and English. Sophia: Universitetsko Izdatelstvo "Sv. Kliment Ochridski," 2013, 390-403; "The Monstrous Goddess:

iconography appear in early historic religions, such as those of Egypt and Mesopotamia, it has been theorized that the figurines represent powerful divine female figures in the Neolithic cultures of Europe and the Near East. The "stiff white nude" figures of the Cyclades, Anatolia, and the Balkans may be death figures, but a pregnant Cycladic figure demonstrates that the Goddess serves regeneration as well as death.[63] Early historic textual evidence of this may be found in the Sumerian *Descent of Inanna*, where the Underworld Goddess and Goddess of death, Ereshkigal, is in the process of giving birth.[64] Just as the more ancient figures, Medusa too is winged, and she has snaky hair: that is, she embodies both the serpentine and the avian aspects of the Neolithic bird/snake Goddess, even though she does not have these characteristics in her earliest depictions.

The bird/snake Goddess represents the continuum of birth, life, death, rebirth. The realms of the bird and snake cover all of the worlds; the realm of the bird is the heavens, while waterbirds also occupy the waters. That of the snake is the earth and Underworld, and likewise water snakes occupy the waters. Both bird and snake embody graphic depictions of birth, since both are oviparous. Both creatures are graphic depictions of regeneration as well, since birds molt and snakes shed their skin. In Neolithic Europe, death and rebirth were tied together in the tomb which served as a ritual place for rebirth: the tomb was also the womb.[65] In her death

---

The Degeneration of Ancient Bird and Snake Goddesses into Historic Age Witches and Monsters." Papers in honor of the 90th Birthday of Marija Gimbutas. *Institute of Archaeomythology* (IAM) Journal, Volume 7. Sebastopol, California: Institute of Archaeomythology, 2011, 181-202.

[63] Marble pregnant Cycladic figure, British Museum No. GR 1932-10.181; 2800-2300 BCE.

[64] The text is a Sumerian fragment; see Samuel Noah Kramer, "Cuneiform Studies and the History of Literature: The Sumerian Sacred Marriage Texts," *Proceedings of the American Philosophical Society* 107.6 (1963): 511, lines 227-228; 232-233.

[65] See Marija Gimbutas, *The Living Goddesses*, edited and supplemented by Miriam Robbins Dexter (Berkeley/Los Angeles: University of California Press, 1999), 55-71.) See also Joan Marler, "An Archaeological Investigation of the

aspect, a Goddess such as Medusa turns people to stone—a form of death, since all human activity ceases for those thus ossified.

Read against the iconographies of the bird/snake goddesses, one can identify ways in which the Underworld Goddess, the death Goddess, gives birth to life. Like Ereshkigal, with her leeky hair, Medusa with her snaky hair is also a birth-giver. But in Medusa's case, she gives birth as she is dying, whereas in the earlier, Sumerian myth the process of death led to regeneration; the Goddess of the Underworld did not have to die in the process of giving birth; she who presided over death presided over rebirth. The winged snake Goddess, before her head is severed by Perseus, is whole; in prehistory she would have been a Goddess of all of the worldly realms. When Medusa's head is severed, she becomes disembodied. Disembodied wisdom is very dangerous. Hence, she becomes monstrous. It is her chthonic self which the Classical world acknowledges: Medusa becomes the snaky-haired severed head, a warning to all women to hide their powers, their totalities. This fearsome aspect goes two ways: she can destroy, but she also brings protection.

In patriarchal societies, the conception of life and death is often seen to be linear rather than circular. Because of a societal fear of death, death figures in patriarchal Indo-European cultures became horrific. Further, in these societies both the feminine divine and the mortal female became subjugated to the males and devalued.[66] Many Indo-European female monsters carry bird and snake iconography. Baltic witches, *raganas*, take the shape of crows, and they have snakes in their hair.[67] The Roman poet Vergil, in the *Aeneid*, gives snaky associations to Furies, Dirae, Sirens, and

---

Gorgon," *ReVision*, vol. 25 (1) (2002): 19.
[66] See Miriam Robbins Dexter, *Whence the Goddesses: A Source Book* (New York: Pergamon. Athene Series 1990).
[67] See Gimbutas, *The Living Goddesses*, 205: "Ragana...carried the energy of a snake; if a Ragana died, you might see her hair curl, like a Gorgon's, into snakes, and little snakes crawl out of her mouth."

Harpies. Many of these fearsome figures are winged as well. Medusa was one of many monstrous figures who received this iconography.

The wings and snakes may have been late additions to the portrayal of Medusa, but they are nonetheless a natural concomitant of the ferocious death Goddess. Wings were added to Medusa's iconography ca. 800 BCE, by the Greeks;[68] later on, she was described as winged in text as well. In the portrayal of the Medusa from Miletus, Medusa is associated with snakes but she is not snaky herself. Nonetheless, she accrued the iconography of the Neolithic bird and snake Goddess, the Great Goddess of birth, death, and regeneration.

The Near Eastern Demon Figure Humbaba

Part of Medusa's iconography and myth was borrowed from the ancient Near East, and this forms an important component of her composite character. In ancient Mesopotamia, in the "Epic of Gilgamesh," the hero (and perhaps first Sumerian king) Gilgamesh fights the demon Humbaba and beheads him,[69] just as later the Greek hero Perseus fights and beheads the Gorgon, Medusa.[70]

---

[68] A.L. Frothingham, "Medusa, Apollo, and the Great Mother," *American Journal of Archaeology* 15 (3) (1911): 364; Clark Hopkins, "Assyrian Elements in the Perseus-Gorgon story," *American Journal of Archaeology* 38 (1934): 344, 358.

[69] Although the Assyrian version of the epic was written ca. 700 BCE, there are Akkadian and Old Babylonian versions as well. At least some of the epic seems to be based upon a Sumerian version. Thus, the epic dates back to at least the beginning of the second millennium BCE. See James B. Pritchard, ed., *Ancient Near Eastern Texts Relating to the Old Testament* (*ANET*), Third Edition. (Princeton, New Jersey: Princeton University Press, 1969), 72-73. For various recensions of the poem, see Pritchard, *ANET*, 73-99. The name of the demon is given as Humbaba and Huwawa in the different tablets.

[70] The slaying of the demon, or demonized figure, may be a motif particular to patriarchal societies. In the myths of the matriarchal Minangkabau, demonized figures (in this case, chaotic male-centered thieves) are subdued by the hero (who may be a double of the queen's son) and, rather than being slain, are convinced to accept the Minangkabau social customs, the *Adat*, and are assimilated into the society. This is a culture of nurturing rather than violence.

The severed head of Humbaba may be a prototype for Medusa's head, severed by Perseus, a motif borrowed by the Greeks during the Orientalizing period, beginning in the late eighth century BCE. Several Mesopotamian sites contained terracotta relief plaques of grimacing faces framed by S-shaped furrows. A seal from Mitanni, dating to ca. 1450 BCE, may depict the detached head of Humbaba.[71] Cyprian art borrowed this iconography as well, and Greek art may have borrowed from both. This motif found its way to Sparta by the eighth or seventh centuries BCE, introduced to Sparta by the Phoenicians.[72] Both Gilgamesh and Perseus employ the Assyrian-Cyprian sickle or harpé for the beheading. At least by 698 BCE—around the time Hesiod was composing the *Theogony*—the Assyrians met the Greeks, when Sennacherib invaded Cilicia. Assyrian power grew during the seventh century, and Assyrian art exerted a direct influence upon the Greek artistic movement.[73] Further, the story of the Gorgon-slaying finds its way into Greek art and myth at a time when the Gilgamesh story—including his beheading of Humbaba—seems very popular in Assyrian texts and art.[74]

Humbaba, just as Medusa, was represented full-face—rather than with face in profile—with legs in profile. He is often represented by his head alone—again similarly to Medusa. Humbaba was portrayed with grimacing mouth, and with two rows of teeth. When full-bodied, he was frequently depicted in the *knielaufen* or bent-knee pose. Medusa assumes both the *knielaufen* pose and the full-face representation. There is a beautiful bent-knee Gorgon on the Western pediment of the Artemis temple in Corfu, dating to ca. 590-580 BCE.

See Peggy Reeves Sanday, *Women at the Center: Life in a Modern Matriarchy* (Ithaca/London: Cornell University Press, 2002), 40-44.
[71] Jane Burr Carter, "The Masks of Ortheia," *American Journal of Archaeology* 91 (1987): 361, footnote 25.
[72] Carter, "The Masks of Ortheia," 362.
[73] Hopkins, "Assyrian Elements in the Perseus-Gorgon story," 345.
[74] Hopkins, "Assyrian Elements in the Perseus-Gorgon story," 357.

The Medusa on this pediment is nine feet tall; her waist is cinched with serpents, and there are only a couple of discrete snakes in her hair. She appears with a lion and with her children, Pegasus and Chrysaor. This bent-knee posture may have a shamanic connection. Indic sky-dancers take this pose,[75] as does the Goddess Kālī and the Irish Kiltinan Sheela na gig. In Bulgaria, there is a 'crooked dance,' danced by women in women's initiation rituals: this may be the dancing version of the bent-knee position, which was probably active dance rather than static stance.[76]

---

[75] See Miranda Shaw, *Passionate Enlightenment: Women in Tantric Buddhism* (Princeton, New Jersey: Princeton University Press, 1994).

[76] Anna Shturbanova and Anna Ilieva, Bulgarian folklorists, personal communication (June, 2004); Anna Ilieva and Anna Shturbanova, "Some Zoomorphic Images in Bulgarian Women's Ritual Dances in the Context of Old European Symbolism," translated by Albena Manafska; in Joan Marler, ed., *From the Realm of the Ancestors: Essays in Honor of Marija Gimbutas* (Manchester,

Iconographically, Humbaba's head was placed over thresholds to guard the inhabitants—an apotropaic function similar to Medusa's. The Medusa head was placed on soldiers' shields, over doorways, as antefixes on roofs, on doors of ovens and kilns, and on Athena's aegis. Many of these Medusa antefixes can be found today, in museums all over the world.

Humbaba's role in the texts was both protective and ferocious. He was protector of the cedars of the forest—and particularly of the sanctuary of Irmini (Ishtar) in the forest, frightening human beings

---

Connecticut, Knowledge Ideas and Trends, 1997), 237-246. See Miriam Robbins Dexter and Victor H. Mair, "Apotropaia and Fecundity in Eurasian Myth and Iconography: Erotic Female Display Figures," in Karlene Jones-Bley, Angela della Volpe, Martin Huld, and Miriam Robbins Dexter, eds., *Proceedings of the Sixteenth Annual UCLA Indo-European Conference, 2004* (Washington, DC: Institute for the Study of Man. Journal of Indo-European Studies Monograph No. 50, 2005), 97-121; *Sacred Display: Divine and Magical Female Figures of Eurasia.* Miriam Robbins Dexter and Victor H. Mair. Amherst, New York: Cambria Press, 2010.

in order to keep them out of the forest.[77] Humbaba could be malevolent or benevolent—similarly to the Goddess Ishtar herself, the Goddess who could cause fruitfulness or barrenness, and who could give birth or bring death.

The Horse

Medusa was depicted as a horse. A Boeotian geometrical-age vase (ca. 650 BCE) portrays Medusa in relief as a centauresse, with the hindquarters of a horse emerging from her lower back.[78] A vase from Rhodes (sixth century BCE) as well as a red-figured amphora from Naples, depict Medusa with a horse's head.[79]

Although we are not told so explicitly in text, when the "dark-blue-maned" one, Poseidon, rapes Medusa, she has become a mare, and that is why she can give birth to a foal, Pegasus. That is, she was the horse as well as the mother of the horse, just as she was the winged one, as well as the mother of the winged horse. She is beheaded—killed—in a ritualistic manner. She thus may be the Greek version of the sacrificed mare in the Indo-European horse-sacrifice, the ritual affirming the Indo-European kingship[80]—that is, she may be an Indo-Europeanization of a pre-Indo-European female figure. The sacrifice of Medusa may also reflect shamanic sacrifice.[81] As

---

[77] Hopkins, "Assyrian Elements in the Perseus-Gorgon story," 346, 357.

[78] See Wilk, *Medousa: Solving the Mystery of the Gorgon*, 36, Figure 3.9.

[79] Gershonson, "The Beautiful Gorgon and Indo-European Parallels," 377. The horse's head had an apotropaic function. In the Roman ritual of the *October Equus*, after a chariot race, the head and tail of the victorious right-hand horse were cut off. The head was then nailed to the wall of a sacred place and it was supposed to protect the people whose city it overlooked. (Gershonson, 379)

[80] See Miriam Robbins Dexter, "The Hippomorphic Goddess and Her Offspring," *Journal of Indo-European Studies* 18 (3-4) (1990): 285-307. As the sacrificed horse, Medusa can be compared to other Indo-European hippomorphic Goddesses: the Old Irish Macha, the Welsh Rhiannon, and the Greek Demeter Erinys. Just as Medusa gives birth at the moment she is decapitated, so the Old Irish third Macha dies at the moment of victory in a race against horses, giving birth to a boy and a horse.

[81] On shamanistic elements and motifs from the myths of Medusa see Ileen

Medusa's head is severed from her body, so her wisdom is severed from her physical self, her sexuality. She has slept with Poseidon and given birth to the horse, Pegasus, and to Chrysaor—but as soon as she fulfills the functions of Mother she becomes a disembodied head. She is frozen in her persona of death.

Viewing the Greek Medusa

By the seventh century BCE, artists began to portray the whole body of Medusa, rather than just the head. It is at this time that we first find the story of Perseus slaying a ferocious, monstrous Medusa in Greek literature, in Hesiod's *Theogony*. However, if we take into consideration a broader chronological spectrum of iconography, we find ferocious female figures dating to the early Neolithic period.

Medusa's iconography grew with time. She grew wings (this rather early), a lolling tongue, and the tusks of a wild boar. The boar's tusks relate her to the death Goddess. There are no Assyrian parallels for Medusa's protruding tongue.[82] Sometimes she is bearded.[83] On the Thracian Kul Oba phiale, Medusa appears with heads of lions.[84] The lions also relate Medusa to Near Eastern Goddesses connected with lions: Inanna, Ishtar, Cybele, and others, and to female figures

---

Brennan Root, *Redeeming the Gorgon: Reclaiming the Medusa Function of Psyche*. (Ph.D. Dissertation, Pacifica Graduate Institute, 2007), 197-201.

[82] Some scholars believe that the Egyptian god Bes, who has a protruding tongue, was a precursor to Medusa. However, there were Neolithic European female figures as well with protruding tongues. See Gimbutas 1999: 24, Figure 1, from the Sesklo culture of Neolithic Thessaly, Northern Greece, dating from 6000-5800 BCE. This head has fangs (compare these to the later boar's tusks of Medusa), large round eyes, a large tongue, and a checkerboard design on its forehead. See also Gimbutas (1989): figure 323, a female figure from South Rumania; ca. 4500 BCE. She has spiral eyes and a large mouth; she holds her shriveled left hand to her lower lip or tongue.

[83] See the bearded Gorgon in Garber and Vickers, *The Medusa Reader*, figure 4. (510-500 BCE; detail of a kylix.)

[84] Compare the way in which Euripides portrays the "barbarian" Medea as a lioness (Euripides. *Medea* 187 *et passim*).

appearing as early as the earliest Upper Palaeolithic, for example, in Chauvet cave. Female display figures are represented with lions from the Upper Palaeolithic Aurignacian period through the Neolithic and Bronze ages.[85] Among the ancient Scythians and Thracians as well, Medusa figures were popular iconographic subjects.[86] In fact, in one Thracian tomb excavated in 2004, the Goliama Kosmatka burial mound near Shipka, in the Bulgarian Valley of the Thracian kings, there has been found a most interesting symbolic burial. There was a corridor with three chambers; in the first, there was a horse sacrifice. The second chamber was round, with a beehive roof. The third and inmost chamber, dug into a granite block weighing more than 60 tons, was shaped like a sarcophagus. A symbolic burial was made in this chamber (in another chamber was found the burial of King Seuthus III), which contained golden objects weighing more than 700 grams. There was a ritual bed molded out of the granite, and at its head was placed a piece of a door on which was sculpted a figure of Medusa; this door was covered with a snake skin,[87] a potent symbol of regeneration.

Female figures similar to Medusa existed in Eastern and Southeast Europe. She may be compared to the earlier Sumerian Underworld Goddess Ereshkigal, as I discussed above. She may also be

---

[85] See *Sacred Display: New Findings*. Miriam Robbins Dexter and Victor H. Mair. *Sino-Platonic Papers*. (http://sino-platonic.org. September, 2013); "Felines, Apotropaia, and the Sacred 'V': Evolution of Symbols Associated with Divine and Magical Female Figures." 2015. *Papers Presented at the International Symposium, From Symbols to Signs, Suceava, Romania, 2-5 September, 2014. In Memory of Klaus Schmidt,* Constantin-Emil Ursu, Adrian Poruciuc, and Cornelia-Magda Lazarovici, eds. Suveava, Romania: Muzeul Bucovinei Suceava, Academia Română-Filiala Iaşi - Institutul de Arheologie Iaşi, Institute of Archaeomythology Sebastopol, Editura Karl A. Romstorfer, pp. 295-316.
[86] See Ellen Reeder, ed., *Scythian Gold: Treasures from Ancient Ukraine* (New York: Harry N. Abrams, Inc., 1999); see also Ivan Marazov, "Iconographies Archaïsantes – Nostalgies des Origines," *Méditerranées* 26-27 (= *Studia Pontica*) (2001): 15-50.
[87] Ivan Marazov (Bulgarian archaeologist and philologist), Personal Communication, 2005; I thank him for bringing me to this tomb in June of 2005.

compared to the Indic Goddess Kālī, the British and Irish Sheela na gigs, and to the Indic Lajjā Gaurī figures who bring good fortune to the temples in which they reside.[88] All of these figures, just as Medusa, belong to Indo-European cultures. But of all of these figures, only Medusa was viewed as a monster, and only Medusa needed to be decapitated and destroyed.

Interpreting Medusa
I believe that Medusa was a synthesis of the Near Eastern male demon-spirit and the Neolithic European Goddess of the Life Continuum, the processes of birth, death, and rebirth. However, she is not just a synthesis of these elements; she remains frozen in her death-aspect, a corpse. Her apotropaic face is a death-mask. But indeed, it is not truly possible to separate the most ancient Goddesses of the life continuum—of birth, death, and rebirth—into a Goddess of life and a Goddess of death. For this reason, historic avatars of the death Goddesses such as the Sumerian/Akkadian-Babylonian/Hebrew Lil/Lilitu/Lilith and Ereshkigal are also voracious in their life-affirming sexuality. They represent love and life as well as death and the Underworld—as does Medusa.

Earlier, I referred to the concept of the tomb as womb; the view that burial monuments were often the sites of rituals involving the concept of regeneration. This raises the possibility of seeing Medusa's gaping mouth of death as the vulva, the cave through which we reach the Underworld, which may be compared to the womb of the birth-mother. In this sense, Medusa is shaman as well, arbiter between this world and the Otherworld.

However, the head as vulva can be terrifying to a male, evoking both the fear of decapitation and castration,[89] and the fear of

---

[88] For comparisons of Medusa with these similar figures throughout Europe and Asia see Dexter and Mair, *Sacred Display: Divine and Magical Female Figures of Eurasia*.

[89] Although psychologists and mythologists frequently have identified the snake,

overpowering female sexuality. The young Irish hero Cú Chulainn and the Greek hero, Bellerophon, responded with fear when they were exposed to large numbers of women who lifted up their skirts. An abundance of female nakedness can overcome even the mightiest warrior. [90] Early psychoanalytical interpretations of Medusa echo this tradition of gynophobia. Sigmund Freud interweaves the story of Medusa with his theory of the castration complex. According to Freud, "to decapitate = to castrate. The terror of Medusa is thus a terror of castration that is linked to the sight of something." [91] Freud believed that the snakes upon Medusa's head were derived from the castration complex. The snakes "replace the penis." Further, "the sight of Medusa's head makes the spectator stiff with terror... becoming stiff means an erection." [92] However, Freud believed that the decapitated head/castrated genitals are so terrifying because they represent "the terrifying genitals of the Mother."[93] This is rather confused thinking. The Hungarian psychoanalyst Sándor Ferenczi (1873-1933) believed that the Medusa head represents the female genitals: "the head of Medusa is the terrible symbol of the female genital region... the phantom itself is the frightful impression made on the child by the penisless (castrated) genital," but in time his point of view became somewhat less patriarchal. [94] The Jungian psychologist, Erich Neumann, also associated the head of Medusa with "the

---

an epiphany of the Neolithic European Goddess of the Life Continuum, as phallic, Judy Grahn, in *Blood, Bread, and Roses: How Menstruation Changed the World* (Boston: Beacon Press, 1993), 186, perhaps more correctly, describes Medusa: "her hair writhing with vaginal snakes."

[90] See Dexter, *Whence the Goddesses: A Source Book*, 160-161.

[91] Sigmund Freud, "Medusa's Head" (original article 1922; published posthumously in 1940) in Garber and Vickers, *The Medusa Reader*, 84-85.

[92] *Ibid.*

[93] *Ibid.*

[94] Sándor Ferenczi, "On the Symbolism of the Head of Medusa." (original article 1923) in Garber and Vickers, *The Medusa Reader*, 87. On the other hand, Ferenczi, after working with many patients who claimed childhood sexual abuse, came to believe that they were telling the truth, and this led to a break with Freud, who believed that such people had fantasized their abuses.

womb in its frightening aspect."[95] He connects the protruding tongue with the phallus, as also the serpents, and he identifies Medusa as the "Terrible Mother." Again, most of these psychologists, Freudian or Jungian, connect the feminine with fear.

Modern Psychological Theories Regarding Medusa

Many modern scholars seem to think that Medusa petrified only men. For example, Jean-Pierre Vernant[96] writes that he knows of no occasion when Medusa engages with a female figure. However, in Pindar, Perseus, through the Medusa-head, turned all of the inhabitants of the island of Seriphus, men and women alike, into stone. Later, Lucan, in the *Pharsalia*, tells us that whole tribes of Ethiopians (Aethiopum totae... gentes. *Pharsalia* 9.651) turned to statues upon beholding Medusa. Although we have not heard from ancient female authors on the subject of Medusa, it is likely that both ancient women and men feared Medusa, whereas many modern women seem to identify with her. Hélène Cixous echoes this belief that the Gorgon does not petrify women; she says "You only have to look at the Medusa straight on to see her. And she's not deadly. She's beautiful, and she's laughing."[97]

Many women have identified with the grimace and the rage of Medusa. May Sarton identifies the Medusa-face as the face of her own frozen rage.[98] Emily Culpepper speaks out of her own experience: "The Gorgon has much vital, literally life-saving information to teach women about anger, rage, power, and the release of the determined aggressiveness sometimes needed for

---

[95] Erich Neumann, "The Origins and History of Consciousnessness" (original article 1949), in Garber and Vickers, *The Medusa Reader*, 96-97.
[96] Jean-Pierre Vernant, "In the Mirror of Medusa," in Garber and Vickers, *The Medusa Reader*, 230, note 22.
[97] Hélène Cixous, "The laughter of the Medusa" in Garber and Vickers, *The Medusa Reader*, 133 (original article 1975).
[98] May Sarton, "The Muse as Medusa" in Garber and Vickers, *The Medusa Reader*, 107-108 (original article 1971).

survival."[99] Patricia Klindienst Joplin tells us why the artist is drawn to Medusa: "Behind the victim's head that turns men to stone may lie the victim stoned to death by men... if Medusa has become a central figure for the woman artist to struggle with, it is because, herself a silenced woman, she has been used to silence other women."[100] Many artists have identified with the rage of Medusa. The Italian scholar and artist, Cristina Biaggi, who now works in the United States, incorporated her studies of prehistory and ancient history and myth into a powerful fiberglass sculpture, "Raging Medusa" (2000). The sculpture is 5.5 feet in diameter and weighs 98 pounds. (See page 52.)

Feminist theologian Catherine Keller insightfully analyzes the myth of Medusa and the unheroic "hero" Perseus.[101] However, she believes that it is only in the Perseus-Athena constellation that Medusa becomes the "Terrible Mother." Otherwise, Medusa represents the "Great Goddess," and her power is "life-giving and generative."[102] The power of the Neolithic bird/snake Goddess, where Medusa has her roots, is indeed life-giving, but Medusa has already changed in her earliest Greek source, Homer, who portrays the Gorgon (not yet individuated into Medusa and two immortal sisters) as a fearsome, bodiless head in the Underworld, but one not yet linked with either Perseus or Athena.

Annis Pratt, who writes on mythology and archetypes in women's fiction, also gives a feminist interpretation of the Medusa-myth; she tells us, "The Medusa archetype has certainly accreted many layers of gynophobic response since its adoption by the Greeks."[103] Pratt

---

[99] Emily Culpepper, "Ancient Gorgons: a Face for Contemporary Women's Rage" in Garber and Vickers, *The Medusa Reader*, 241 (original article 1986).
[100] Patricia Klindienst Joplin, "Rape and Silence in the Medusa Story," in Garber and Vickers, *The Medusa Reader*, 201-202 (original article 1984).
[101] Catherine Keller, *From a Broken Web* (Boston: Beacon Press, 1986), 50-73. I thank Carol P. Christ for this reference.
[102] Keller, *From a Broken Web*, 60.
[103] Annis Pratt, *Dancing with Goddesses* (Bloomington: Indiana University Press,

describes many Romantic and Victorian poets who describe and relate to Medusa, usually with some horror. This echoes the male Greco-Roman interpretation of the snake, an interpretation which is more pejorative than earlier depictions and interpretations.

Conclusion

Although Medusa may be of use to modern feminists, providing an ancient locus for modern rage, it is important to see that the raging head of Medusa has lost the fullness of the original powers of the Neolithic Goddess of the Life Continuum. The Greek Medusa is different from her sisters across time and space. Whereas the Neolithic Goddess is a powerful arbiter of birth, death, and rebirth, she has been transformed in Greek from a Goddess of the life continuum to a dead head. Although Medusa is still sexual in the Greek material—she has sex with Poseidon in a meadow and gives birth to twins—she becomes more closely associated with death than with life. She becomes feared and she therefore must be murdered. Perhaps if one kills death, then the living somehow won't have to die—at least in mythical time.

Medusa continues to be viewed as protective and apotropaic— warding off evil, warding off the enemy—and even healing in the Greek tradition, but she has also lost her power. It is thus important to pay attention to her beneficent aspects: the fact that half of her blood is healing, and that images of her head are used to protect buildings of multiple functions within the Greco-Roman sphere; so protective is she considered to be that her head was buried near the Argive market-place. Medusa is magical. She reminds us that we must not take the female "monster" at face value; that we must weigh not only her beneficent against her maleficent attributes, but we must also take into consideration the world view and the sociopolitical stance of the cultures which create her, fashioning the demonic female as scapegoat for the benefit and comfort of the patriarchal members of their societies.

1994), 11.

The Gorgon Medusa
Sudie Rakusin

What Happened to You, Medusa?
Barbara Ardinger, Ph.D.

Medusa, what happened to you?
You and your sisters were filled with such grace,
you were all fair of face, with gentle eyes,
you were a priestess of the warrior/wisdom maiden—
what wisdom did you own?
But why did you lie with the sea god
and what did he tell you?
Did you hear only a seducer's deceiving words,
or did he tell you secrets of sea and land and earthquake?
What did you learn?

Medusa, what is the source of your rage?
Is it betrayal—
did you betray the warrior/wisdom maiden,
or were you betrayed by her?
And what did the hero do to you?
How were you hidden from the sun?
Are you, like all who see you now, threatened
by the vipers that crown you?
Who turned you into embodied anger,
and why do men say you can kill with a single glance?

What mysteries do you—and your writhing snakes—
have to speak to us today?
Did those snakes used to be sparks of goddess
flashing round your head?
What happened to you, Medusa?

Ave Medusa
Jeanne K. Raines

Medusa: When the Soldiers

Susan Hawthorne

the desert is in your mouth
with your eyes you terrify
that was not how you were
anger stirred you

when the soldiers came
they punished you
and every woman they found
gods joined in the pack rape

you promised revenge
not once but for all time
against those who poisoned you
with their violence

when the soldiers beheaded you
you transformed into a winged horse
flying across the sky
wielding sunbeams

your face created terror in men
you are a mask and more
turned inward mirroring
the viewer's soul

when the soldiers spilt your blood
where your severed head fell
corals turned red   we wear
these necklaces in memory of you

Raging Medusa
Cristina Biaggi, Ph.D.

The RAGING MEDUSA's face was inspired by the singer Maria Callas singing Norma at the Met and hitting a high C. She represents the rage of women and the Earth herself with patriarchy and the deleterious effects of patriarchy the world over.

Calling Medusa In
Jane Meredith

IF WE WERE TO LOOK at our childhoods, really look at the horror of them, we would turn to stone.

As we get to know our friends, the layers strip back between us and another version is revealed. The drunken parents who forgot their middle child's birthday. The mother too depressed to get out of bed, or who laid on the couch crying for a year. The fathers who were absent, violent, or addicts—or the stepfathers who took their places and were violent, alcoholics, rapists. Having the wrong clothes at school, or no lunches, having to pretend everything was all right while at home terrible scenes were enacted weekly, monthly, daily. The danger, the fear, the wounds inflicted physically, mentally, emotionally, spiritually.

If we were to really look, to open our eyes and see what was there, as an observer or maybe to reclaim it through the eyes of the four-year-old girl hiding terrified in her room, hoping somehow the waves of shouting and crashing pass over her; the toddler who couldn't be taken to hospital during her epileptic fit because all the adults were so high they couldn't drive; the seven-year-old struggling to be self-sufficient; the ten-year-old looking after younger siblings; the teenager trying to stay in school while caring for a parent who was alcoholic, disabled, depressed; the daughter not fighting off her brother, or father, or cousin, or uncle—believing that it kept the family together, or because she wouldn't be believed or would be blamed... the children put into foster care to be neglected, abused, traumatised by unrelated adults or shifted endlessly one home to the next. If we were to really see all of this we would surely turn to stone in horror, outrage, disbelief, of utter heart-breaking tragedy that cannot, cannot be borne.

Rape. How many, how endlessly many of us carry that story? Carry it in our flesh, our memory, our very cells recording the violation the near-obliteration of our selves, our fragile child-bodies, our resilient child-minds, the selves of us formed in torment and still this endless desire to survive. Rape by fathers, brothers, uncles, grandfathers—how many incest stories have I heard by now? Sexual abuse by older siblings, cousins, gangs, sometimes mothers even; violence and horror and deep levels of manipulation practiced casually at the tortured edge of life and death, those children learning deep within them how to live on the edge how to somehow grow up despite all that; this would turn us to stone if we really looked at it. The statistics—up to one in three girls, up to one in six boys (this was in Australia in 1999, somehow, I don't believe it's any less in 2017)—experienced sexual abuse of some kind before their eighteenth birthday. Do you feel the chill in your flesh setting in; your thinking beginning to grind to a halt; your movements slowing, stuttering, the breath coming more shallowly? We're starting to turn to stone, reading or writing this, thinking about it.

Then there was the ordinary, almost dull level of humiliation and defeat inseparable from childhood. That casual, merciless way we were subjected to the power of others in the everyday, dragged along the street crying with hiccups, face a mess and unable to coordinate my feet under the stress; being told-off publicly, humiliated in front of our friends or family; the way it was assumed we couldn't hear or wouldn't understand when they discussed our faults; the preferencing when they gazed with eyes and words of praise at our brothers or sisters and glazed past us—how do any of us come out of it as half-way presentable human beings? Remember that they lied, neglected and beat us; remember that they did not rise in our defense when we were attacked outside our homes but instead brushed it off or told us to grow up, which desperately we tried to do. Remember how dangerous life was. We were lucky to survive.

We may have turned to stone somewhere along the way, in some subtle shifting manner so we don't fully realise it. We just block that part of our lives out, build a wall or two. Encase ourselves in a fort, a high tower, an underground bunker. Stone is good for all that, walls and towers and bunkers. When our friends start to reveal their childhood miseries and shames we retreat, back behind our own wall and shore up the chinks, so the horror doesn't seep through. It's contaminating. I can't hear about your nightmare without remembering my own. So, I don't want to hear. Not that I can forget my own—it visits me in a hundred ways; at night in the landscape of dream, or during the day when I see a child encased in misery in the street or supermarket and sneaking into my relationships or even in the memory of how I sometimes was with my own child.

I'm looking at my childhood and I'm in the process of turning into stone. Or turning into something—maybe stone is just a transition point and then I'll erupt, spewing lava, molten stone, magma and it will be so fierce I'll cover everything with it and even the memories will melt.

I read Tarot cards for a young woman, seventeen maybe, and the cards were horrible. I noticed her nervousness, and in her hands, she was wearing a piece of cheap jewellery where a ring is attached to a chain that links to a bracelet around the wrist. A slave bracelet, it's called. When I asked why the cards were so dreadful she told me her father came into her room at night and sexually abused her—raped her, a couple of times a week, had for years, maybe five or six years. I told her the name of her bracelet, she fumbled with it, trying to get it off. I asked why she didn't leave and she said she had a younger sister, maybe even two of them, I forget the details now. She said as long as she stayed, they were safe from him. I asked, "how do you know?"—and saw a new level of horror enter her life. I hope she did something. I gave her phone numbers to call. I hope I reflected her horror enough to get her attention, that snakes rose up out of my hair, in her eyes and she was spurred into action. This was not the only time I heard that story.

My story isn't that bad. But isn't that the way we diminish the grief of it, measuring against others and saying, oh well it isn't as bad as that. We survived after all and mostly we had homes and went to school and mostly our lives are better, now. Shored up with all that stone, perhaps, and the way we let our eyes glaze over and stopped thinking feeling being almost just barely breathing until it passed over us, like a storm or through us and then we came back into our bodies though our bodies weren't the same any longer—that cortisol still streaking through us changing the way we dealt with shock and pain, numbing us like stones to our own feelings, our own sense of danger til we couldn't properly tell, any longer, which situations were good for us and which weren't, we were drawn to danger maybe for the thrill, that's what it took to spike our dulled emotions into feeling something or—even more sinister—for the familiarity of it.

This is all just in the ordinary suburbs of civilised Western life. This does not take into account actual war, genocide, child soldiers, slavery, child brides, genital mutilation, child prostitution, most of the world really. Medusa—where are you? When the patriarchy cut off your head was it to prevent your telling these stories, the stories of women and children and drawing all eyes to the horror of them? Was it to take your terrible powers and turn them onto those who are already the victims? To stop the power of serpents and stone that paralyse the perpetrators and let the innocent transform their suffering? When we reclaim Medusa's heritage what shall we turn to stone? And then we shall slither free, out of those cracks in the walls or from under the foundations, shedding our skins as we go and becoming bright and beautiful. We will shed those childhood skins, the shapes of our suffering, and with our knowledge, we will become healers and artists and activists.

Perhaps you were not one of those children. Maybe you had an ordinary safe loving nurturing amazing or just uneventful childhood. Can you listen to these stories, watch them playing out in the adult lives of your friends and lovers and not find yourself turning somehow toward stone, the contamination reaching out and into your ears and eyes as you are forced to consider how people treat the smallest amongst us, most helpless, dependent and fragile beings? Do you turn away, refuse to listen or do you try to hold these stories within your largess and if you don't turn to stone, what happens then? Can you convince us we are safe, now, listen long enough to still the demons, step up to the challenges we throw at you, untrusting, unsure? Can you stay present to help weave a different story for us, for those who have been turned to stone, somewhere on the inside?

What would it be like to reclaim these histories and breathe through them, to let them out into the open and not have to carry them with us, like stones on our backs, in our hearts, blocking our eyes and ears and freezing our brains? What would it be like to wield the Medusa power of stones and snakes? Look into my eyes and know the truth of my childhood, of all our childhoods, the wounded ones and I think that's most of us by now; I'm really not sure who there is left to turn into stone. So perhaps it's the institutions, the nuclear family or just the family, the schools that don't notice or can't do anything for the blasted children who inhabit them, the systems of work and economy and poverty and pain that grind down the adults responsible for these small ones til they can't think and can hardly love and have nowhere to turn and no answers and no resources and clearly it's all utterly terrible; what if those institutions turned to stone and we were set free?

Because if we don't turn into stone, or we turn into stone but then we keep turning, there's a transformation, a transition, a snake-like twist and turning—and serpent-like we hiss and rise and maybe strike, paralysing our enemies or maybe we just slither off elsewhere, somewhere more interesting and rub up against a few difficult places and slip our skins and are reborn.

Medusa. Hiss her name out, like snakes. This is the worst, the most terrible thing—and if we can face that and still reach out to each other, if we can look it full in the face as it happens all around us in the houses and supermarkets and families we see on buses in the parks, in our own street and presumably in the houses of our friends and colleagues and our own families, happening still—if we can face it and not be turning into stone then we can strike. Let the serpents rise from my head, many bodied, writhing. Let them call out what they know and mark it as an act of horror, like thoughts that finally have to speak themselves. And shouting, singing into being, let us finally honour this ancient goddess: the mystery of facing terrible truth. Medusa's head was cut off but let us reclaim that—this ancient knowledge: the power to see and know the truth.

Oh Medusa, I'm calling you in. I invoke you. I invoke you into the Royal Commission into Institutional Responses to Child Sexual Abuse, I invoke you into my own life and the lives of my friends, I invoke you into the houses and families of childhoods everywhere. May there be a Royal Commission into the Family. Into childhood abuse in the home. Well might our faces be masks of horror, well might we feel parts of ourselves turning to stone as we confront what awaits us. Feel the shivers down your spine, the hairs rising on your arms and neck. Bring your qualities Medusa—it *is time*. It is time serpents were released and wildness broke the stone face of what is acceptable and we saw behind the masks and those who raise spear or shield against you were struck with the power of truth.

Power
Lizzie Yee

> Male parasitism means males must have access to women. It is the PATRIARCHAL imperative. BUT feminist NO-saying is more than a substantial removal, redirection, reallocation of goods and services because access is one of the faces of POWER. Female denial of male access to females substantially cuts off a flow of benefits, but it has also the form and the full portent of assumption of POWER
>
> —Marilyn Frye—

To Stand Witness
Teri Uktena

THE MEDUSA MYTH has always been a favorite of mine. I mean, it's cool right? As a kid it's a great story like Godzilla vs. Mothra. There is a horrible monster doing horrible monstery things which needs to be vanquished. And there is a hero who looks just like every other guy and he gets help from the pretty gods and he gets all these cool gadgets and he goes out, screws up his courage and defeats the monster. Hurray! Even better, *Clash of the Titans* with Harry Hamlin is a cult classic and the owl Bubo is a delight.

However, I also was bothered by the myth from the very beginning because it made no sense. Rarely was a monster called out as either male or female—it was just monstrous and somewhat assumed to be male (ish?). So why all the angst around this one baddie? Why was she female? Why was that a bad thing? Other monsters were ugly, but their ugliness didn't kill, their actions did. And it really confused me that a girl monster would be powerful and deadly and need to be killed while pretty women were helpless damsels that needed to be saved. And why do they always just weep and allow themselves to be tied to things?

Unfortunately for us, the Medusa myth is alive and well, though not because of any CGI filled remakes. Medusa was a physically beautiful woman. In Ovid's telling this is presented as uncomfortable, not in and of itself, but because she knew she was beautiful and this made everyone around her uncomfortable. There is a subtext to this implying negativity if you fully embody who you are as woman. (*You know*, be too attractive and you attract things you don't want.) Don't be powerful, don't be uppity, don't be who you are, don't be… Poseidon, god of the seas, second most powerful god next to Zeus (his brother) sees her and is attracted to her. He approaches her, comments on her looks, and suggests they make love. She says no. He then forces her into the temple of Athena (who among other things is a staunch virgin with no mother) and rapes her. There are no repercussions for Poseidon. He just leaves afterwards. Athena is enraged, not at him, but at Medusa. Athena turns Medusa's beauty into such horrid ugliness it cannot be looked on because it will turn anyone who sees it into stone. To look at such defilement, such grossness is to become forever its mute stone witness.

I say this myth is alive and well because you can hear it in each woman who comes forward to speak about their experiences with Bill Cosby (who hasn't been charged with any crime). It is retold in each victim that comes forward to speak about Jimmy Savile from the BBC.[104] In each case, a person who was beautiful because they lived, because they existed, because they were a portion of divinity, was taken advantage of in a way which was so destructive they were forever changed. This in itself is a horrible facet of humanity. What is worse, when it became known they had been taken advantage of there was no outrage toward the perpetrator, but outrage at them, the victim. They are turned into a hideous monster who is so dangerous they must be shunned because just looking upon them will destroy mortal man. They are other, they are evil, they are a warning to all who hear the tale, don't be too much, don't be too good, too beautiful, too powerful, too anything. Keep your head down and hopefully you won't be destroyed.

When Anita Sarkeesian says, "One of the most radical things you can do is to actually *believe* women," she's speaking directly to this. That Medusa isn't a monster. She's us. She's someone who has been radically changed by the despicable actions of other beings. Our inability to look at her, to see her, the myth that we will be turned to stone if we see her, is all about fear. It's about what will happen to us if we actually see her for who she has become. This is in part

---

[104] https://en.wikipedia.org/wiki/Jimmy_Savile_sexual_abuse_scandal

the power of the *New York Magazine* cover.105 It's nothing more than a black and white picture of seated women and one empty chair. But when I look at it, I see Medusa in all of her amazing and heart breaking varieties. In this picture I see all of the women I have worked with over the years who have struggled because no one would believe them and people actively worked against their being able to seek help or even validation. I see myself telling my family what happened to me and hearing them respond that I was lying. And I remember one of the most amazing days of my life, when I told my story in the presence of men I had never met and they believed me.

Medusa isn't a story in some book: she's all around us. She's not a monster too ugly to look upon, she's the ugly truth. If we have to look at her through the shield of a magazine photo or stand with our backs to her and look at her through a mirror, then so be it. The time when sending Perseus to kill her would work is ending. It's time to give over this turning to stone business and instead become the heroes that stand witness to what has been done.

---

[105] Moyer, Justin. 35 Bill Cosby accusers on *New York Magazine*'s cover. July 27, 2015.

See No Evil
Caroline Alkonost

Medusa: The Invitation

Maureen Owen

I CAN STILL REMEMBER the first time I heard the story of Medusa. I knew instinctively, that to come with such warnings, Medusa must be incredibly powerful. Instantly intrigued, I started to dig deeper. Over time, as I have come to understand more of the symbolism that sits within this story, a very different understanding has emerged. My sense now is that this is not a story of a monster, it is instead a story of ancient and divine wisdom calling me to reclaim all of who I am as a woman.

The story of Medusa is fundamentally the story of the domination of the patriarchal invaders of mainland Greece over the early goddess culture of North Africa.[106] It is the story of the victory of the masculine principle governed by power and control over the feminine principle, one that saw the sacredness in the everyday, and valued peace, fertility, justice with compassion, equality and transformation.[107] Some scholars believe the story reflects actual events during the reign of King Perseus around 1290 BCE.[108]

When I hear this story, I hear Medusa's invitation urging me to look deeper than the patriarchal version of who she was. At the heart of this invitation, I believe Medusa is calling me into a deeper relationship with myself and the divine. She is urging me to reclaim the intelligence, strength and creativity rooted in the feminine tradition.

This essay is an exploration of this invitation and the key symbolism within Medusa's story that points to this and the elements of the feminine lineage she is urging me to reclaim.

---

[106] Demetra George, 1992, p156.
[107] Lucia Chiavola Birnbaum, 2001, p6.
[108] Demetra George, 1992, p161.

I begin with an examination of her most obvious symbol, the serpents, and then proceed to what I know of the roles she held and what they symbolised. As such, I explore the meaning of what it meant to hold the roles of High Priestess; Goddess; Queen; and Crone.[109]

I have chosen symbolism to guide me on this journey because I know from the earliest times, symbolism has been used to inform human understanding of the cosmos and our place in it. Along with telling us what something represents, symbols also hint at what is missing, what is invisible and what is needed to achieve completion or wholeness.[110] As such, coming to understand the symbolic meaning behind these aspects of Medusa has provided me with vital insights into what has been lost, and what can be reclaimed.

The Serpents
Of all animal symbols, I have learned that the serpent or snake is probably the most significant and complex.[111] Snakes represent the vitality of the energy and consciousness of life in the body and the vitality of spiritual consciousness in the life and in the world.[112] They signify the need to shed our old skin in order to grow and are seen as a symbol of healing, wisdom and transformation.[113] Hence, these themes of needing to shed old identities to grow and heal, to access wisdom and transform, seem core to understanding Medusa and her roles as high priestess, goddess, queen and crone, and her invitation.

The snake also symbolises sacred kundalini energy. Kundalini lies asleep at the base of the spine, until she is awakened, and rises through the chakras, activating each one in turn—eventually

---

[109] Demetra George, 1992, p 155.
[110] Mark O'Connell & Raje Airey, 2011, pp 6–8.
[111] Mark O'Connell & Raje Airey, 2011, p1 86.
[112] Joseph Campbell, 2013, p 120.
[113] Jean Shinoda Bolen, 2004, p 8.

coming out at the crown of the head as enlightenment.[114] I know from my own personal experience, and from my teaching work with the chakras, the incredible transformative power of the chakras. For when we work with the chakras, bringing them into balance, this vital energy can be transmuted into awareness, spirituality and a deeper understanding of life and our place in the universe.[115]

Hence for me, the snakes symbolise the creative and spiritual potential contained within our bodies that can be used and cultivated for healing, wisdom and transformation. It is the potential that Genevieve Paulson, in her book "Evolution in this Lifetime," talks about pushing "each of us toward the goal of enlightenment—knowing the light," the divine within. The symbolism behind Medusa's serpents is essentially about the evolution of the human soul, and so I hear her enticing me to go beyond my current comprehensions of what it means to be human, to know the light, and to become Goddess-like.[116]

The fact that Medusa's snakes cover her head is also significant from the perspective of the chakras. This directly links the snakes to the crown chakra, which is associated with: surrender, trust, universal connectedness, stillness, peace, divinity, wisdom, being part of something bigger, spiritual wisdom, unity, and pure consciousness.[117] It is through the crown chakra that we reach the heights of spirituality and we connect with our indelible and permanent divinity.[118] Thus, the crown of snakes symbolises Medusa's capacity to connect me with my higher purpose, divine guidance and my spiritual path.

---

[114] Jean Shinoda Bolen, 2004, p 30.
[115] Ambika Wauters, 2010, p 16.
[116] Genevieve Lewis Paulson, 2015, p 1.
[117] Maureen Owen, 2016, p 25.
[118] Ambika Wauters, 2010, p 114.

High Priestess

Evidence points to Medusa being a high priestess of Africa—a fact reinforced in her story when we are told she "was the only one of the three sisters who was mortal."[119] From this, I know she is more than just a mythological figure; she actually lived and breathed and walked the earth as I do. For me this reinforces that Medusa is not just a character in an ancient myth—that she has a real substance and an essential truth about her. This truth applies equally to the level of demonisation and devastation she experienced, and the healing, wisdom and transformation she represents—and that I feel her inviting me to reclaim.

Being a high priestess meant that Medusa was a keeper of knowledge, trained in the sacred arts of religious rites, adornment, massage, the practices of healing and divination, and the secret mysteries of sexual union. The role of priestess included initiating men into the deep and secret mysteries of the heart; "awakening them to their spiritual potential;" and channelling their spiritual fire inward and upward along the sacred path of enlightenment.[120] A man who came to her temple would have approached her as the embodiment of the goddess hoping or knowing that through her he might experience the goddess. She "would be his priestess, not a prostitute—a holy woman, not a fallen woman."[121] Thus, I sense Medusa pointing me toward a vastly different understanding of sexuality, my body, and of the spiritual potential of sexual union as a source of spiritual awakening.[122]

I now know that the priestess of the ancient world cultivated kundalini energy to facilitate spiritual awakening. This sits in stark contrast to the conditioning I received that endeavoured to etch deep into my psyche a belief that the path to realisation, fulfilment, and enlightenment was all about denying the body and something

---

[119] Demetra George, 1992, p 153.
[120] Jean Shinoda Bolen, 2004, pp 129-134 & Sharon Rose, 2002, p 139.
[121] Jean Shinoda Bolen, 2004, pp 129-134 & Sharon Rose, 2002, p 139.
[122] Sera Beak, 2013, p 86.

a woman could never ever aspire to. Hence, I sense Medusa urging me to truly comprehend that my female body is a receptacle and transmitter of divine energy.[123] I hear her urging me to question the messages I have been fed about my body, urging me to reclaim the mystical affiliation with the archetypal feminine and the sacredness of my body. This sacred invitation is to know myself fully as woman and therefore as goddess—the embodiment of the divine feminine principle.[124]

Goddess

Joseph Campbell holds that the key to understanding the mythology of the goddess is about seeing her as the transformer.[125] And as transformer, the goddess has three functions: "one, to give us life; two, to be the one who receives us in death; and three, to inspire our spiritual, poetic realization."[126] The goddess is the life-force of the universe. She is the innate power—in reality, the power to be conscious, to feel ecstasy; the power of will and desire; the power to know and to act; and the force that inescapably nudges the evolution of human consciousness.[127] As such, the goddess represents the embodiment of the divine within me, and the source of transformation and creative inspiration in my life.[128]

I also know, from my work with the chakras, that the goddess is intrinsically linked to sacred kundalini energy that is nudging me toward the evolution of my consciousness. She is the feminine face of God, the Shakti (the divine feminine) who when awoken begins her journey, from the base of the spine to her beloved Shiva (the divine masculine) who waits for her at the crown chakra. This energy and drive represents the divine marriage, "the union of masculine and feminine principles in the universe and" in me.

---

[123] Sharon Rose, 2002, p 212.
[124] Jean Shinoda Bolen, 2004, pp 68-69.
[125] Joseph Campbell, 2013, p 25.
[126] Joseph Campbell, 2013, p 36.
[127] Sally Kempton, 2013, pp 6-12.
[128] Sera Beak, 2013, p 157.

Medusa reminds me that "the attraction of polarities one for the other—is a fundamental cosmic principle" and it's not just necessary to keep replicating the human species, it is also how I evolve.[129] And so, I sense Medusa urging me to comprehend the importance of this attraction and to understand the significance of the feminine within it. She is urging me to shed the limitations that I have been conditioned with and to receive, grow and evolve into the sacredness of this new understanding.

Queen
I see the queenly aspect of Medusa in how she maintains her sovereignty, despite being cast as a hideous monster. It is here that I see the depth of her strength, integrity and inner authority. Here are a few examples from her story:

1. When her neck was severed, her twin sons sprang forth—Pegasus, the winged moon horse who became a symbol of poetry; and Cryasor, the hero of the golden sword and father of King Geryon of Spain.
2. In the drops of her blood that trickled onto the hot African sands, an oasis grew in the desert.
3. Her blood, given to Asklepius, the God of Healing, bestowed the ability to cure, restore and save lives. His symbol, of a serpent entwined around a rod (associated with healing and medicine), is still used today.
4. And in her ongoing connection with Athena, and with Athena's willingness to always be identified with Medusa, having placed the Gorgon's head over her heart and wearing it for protection.[130]

In all of this, I see Medusa's actions holding true to what I believe she stood for—healing, wisdom and transformation. The outcomes, despite how she has been portrayed by the invading patriarchy, are

---

[129] Teri Degler, 2009, pp 231-232.
[130] Demetra George, 1992, pp 155-158.

defined by Medusa herself and her values, not by those describing her as a hideous monster. As such, I see Medusa urging me to access a new and deeper level of inner authority, to understand who I truly am at my core, urging me to live from this place despite the limitations of our patriarchal society. The more I can enact feminine consciousness in my everyday life—living the truth in my soul, the conviction in my heart, and the wisdom in my body—the more empowered I will become and the more capable I will be effecting the world around me.[131]

Crone

Medusa also embodies the crone aspect of the triple Goddess. The crone is associated with the themes of being timeless, detached, fearless, free, beauty, guide, wisdom, surrender, spontaneity, and paradox.[132] The crone is the woman who has gone through the crossroads in her life and is in a place where she has surrendered her ego demands to a higher will; having accepted her own destiny, she is free and fearless; no longer needing to justify her existence; nor fearing the judgement of others; she has learnt to trust herself.[133] The crone is a mature woman who has a sense of truly being herself.[134] This aspect of Medusa paints a clear picture of the wisdom, power and beauty available to me as mature conscious woman and the prize for undertaking the inner work required to be a crone and step into my full sovereign power.

I also know that the qualities of the crone are not automatically bestowed "following menopause, any more than growing older and wiser go hand in hand."[135] The crone is a potential I can develop, and to do this I need to recognise, practice and listen to it. Accordingly, Medusa is inviting me to look below the surface to shed old ways of perceiving this stage of a woman's life and to grow

---

[131] Sue Monk Kidd, 1996, p 219.
[132] Marion Woodman & Elinor Dickson, 1996, p 10.
[133] Marion Woodman & Elinor Dickson, 1996, p 87 & Woodman, 1983, p 87.
[134] Jean Shinoda Bolen, 2003, p 4.
[135] Jean Shinoda Bolen, 2003, p 8.

into my full creative and spiritual potential. To understand, that until this span of my life is over, I am still in process; in the midst of an unfinished story; and what I say and do makes a difference. This is an invitation to access the fullness of the power and wisdom that is my birthright. For when this potential is activated, I know it will help me to act as a counterbalance to the frenzied ambition, competition and materialism that drives much of the patriarchal world I find myself living in.

Reclaiming

At its core, Medusa's invitation is about reclaiming the divine connection within and the healing, wisdom and transformation that is encoded deep within me. An essential part of reclaiming the divine within seems to be about my willingness to reclaim those parts of myself that I have labelled, or the culture I live in has labelled, as monstrous. These are all the discarded, devalued, unaccepted and disowned aspects of myself that are often referred to as the shadow. Like everyone else, this part of me is the part I like to keep a lid on and hide if I can. I realise now, this process of hiding consumes huge amounts of my psychic energy.[136]

I have also come to learn that the shadow can also "contain the divine, the luscious, beautiful, and powerful aspects of personhood." And for women, especially, the shadow almost always contains very fine aspects of being that are forbidden or given little support in patriarchal culture. To my delight, I now realise that at the bottom of the well in my psyche where I have relegated these disowned aspects of myself also lies "the visionary creator, the astute truth-teller, the far-seer, the one who can speak well of herself without denigration, who can face herself without cringing, and the one who works to perfect her craft."[137] Accordingly, Medusa's invitation is urging me to reclaim the wisdom within because my feminine soul is demanding that I have access to it all.

---

[136] Jean Shinoda Bolen, 1999, p 215.
[137] Clarissa Pinkola Estes, 1992, pp 236-239.

And so, I have come to the end of exploring the invitation and insights that Medusa has offered me. This calling—to come into a deeper relationship with myself and the divine; to reclaim all these parts of myself, the intelligence, strength and creativity that is rooted in the feminine tradition; and to shed old understanding of who I thought I was to access the healing, wisdom and transformation that I now know is encoded into the very core of my being. Medusa has shown me the way home to who I truly am and urged me to awaken the goddess within.

REFERENCES:

Beak, S. 2013, *Red Hot & Holy – A Heretic's Love Story*, Sounds True, Boulder, Colorado.

Birnbaum, L. C. 2001, *Dark Mother – African Origins and Godmother*, iUniverse, Inc, Lincoln. NE.

Bolen, J.S. 1999, *Ring of Power – Symbols and Themes, Love vs Power in Wagner's Ring Cycle and In Us – A Jungian Feminist Perspective*, Nicolas-Hays, Inc. York Beach, Maine.

Bolen, J.S. 2003, *Crones Don't' Whine – Concentrated Wisdom for Juicy Women*, Conari Press, Boston.

Bolen, J.S. 2004, *Crossing to Avalon, 10th Anniversary Edition*, Harper Collins, New York.

Campbell. J. 2013, *Goddesses, Mysteries of the Feminine Divine*, New World Library, Novato, California.

Degler, T. 2009, *The Divine Feminine Fire, Creativity and Your Yearning to Express Your Self,* Dreamriver Flourtown, PA, USA.

George, D. 1992, *Mysteries of the Dark Moon – The Healing Power of the Dark Goddess*, Harper Collins, New York.

Kempton, S. 2013, *Awakening Shakti – The Transformative Power of the Goddesses of Yoga,* Sounds True, Boulder, Colorado.

Monk Kidd, S. 1996, *The Dance of the Dissident Daughter – A Woman's Journey from Christian Tradition to the Sacred Feminine –* Harper Collins, New York.

O'Connell, M and Airey, R. 2011, *The Complete Encyclopedia of Signs & Symbols*, Southwater, Leicestershire.

Owen, M. 2016, *The Wisdom Blueprint*, www.lotusspace.com.au, Brisbane, Australia.

Paulson, G. 2015, *Evolution in this Lifetime A Practical Guide - Kundalini and the Chakras*, Llewellyn Publications, Woodbury, MN.

Pinkola Estes, C. 1992, *Women Who Run With The Wolves – Contacting the Power of the Wild Woman*, Random House, London.

Rose, S. 2002, *The Path of the Priestess – A Guidebook for Awakening the Divine Feminine, Inner Traditions,* Rochester, Vermont.

Wauters, A. 2010, *The Complete Guide to Chakras – Unleash the positive power within*, Barrons, London.

Woodman, M, 1983, *Conscious Femininity – Interviews with Marion Woodman*, Inner City Books, Toronto, Canada.

Woodman, M. & Dickson, E. 1996, *Dancing in the Flames – The Dark Goddess in the Transformation of Consciousness*, Shambhala, Boston.

Oracle
Janet Guastavino

Medusa,
offspring of earth and ocean,
    nurtured by the wellsprings of life.
Serpent tendrils crown you,
    whispering wisdom
        and white noise
        to shield you
        from the taunts of those
        maddened by your power.
Fecund Gaia and Oceanus
course through your veins, and
the curse set upon you
    is a circlet of *enlightenment*.
You speak the Oldest Truths
    and foretell the futures of men,
    who have no stomach to hear them.
For this, you are scorned;
for this, you shall be exalted.

Sisterhood is Subversive
Diane Goldie

My painting, "Sisterhood is Subversive" was inspired by an interview with the wonderful Eartha Kitt where she was being questioned by a male interviewer on compromise. The sexism in his line of questioning was quite apparent and Eartha didn't let this go unnoticed. She stayed strong and fierce, stating her position and using laughter and bold presence to unnerve the 70s chauvinist. I saw a warrior woman, a woman who understood her power and humanity, a woman who had earned her wisdom through a lot of pain but rose up triumphant and ultimately untouchable. She had Medusa spirit. I was so inspired by this interview that I wanted to create a visual symbol to represent her spirit. I was currently working with images of Frida Kahlo, an artist who also pushed gender boundaries and expectations of female behaviour. Something made me pick up a brush and paint snakes over her hair, and this image was born. I immediately realised that if all women could find this spirit within then and held hands in solidarity, Patriarchy would end, hence the slogan *sisterhood is subversive.* Many of my black female friends were struggling to feel included in the mostly white-centered feminist movement so I wanted to focus on a feminist message about sisterhood rather than straight feminism.

The other motto that went with this image was directly inspired by what I saw in Eartha: A woman who loves herself is a dangerous woman. Dangerous to patriarchy of course.

This image forms the back of my most powerful garment, a kimono with big sleeves that forces me to take up space and stand regal, in my power. Every time I wear it, I have a magical interaction with a sister in need of hearing her worth.

Medusa's Nappy Dreads
Luisah Teish

He dared to approach her door with trembling hands and eyes lowered to deliver the document.

It read that her "nappy dread locks" were an "affront and an offense" and violated the company's dress code.

She screamed "fuck you" and shook her head so fiercely that her long black locks slapped his face. He froze for a moment and then stumbled away.

She'd been the bright and beautiful black woman who captured the media's attention. But she'd also refused to worship the gods of Silicon Valley Power, Privilege and Arrogance. And she even dared to blow the whistle on sexual harassment, pollution and worker exploitation. So, they punished her with exile.

She smashed the company computer, sent papers flying and cleared her desk.

Her long black locks caressed her as she slid across the room, to admire her own reflection in the mirror.

Fearless Protector: A Self-Portrait
Alyscia Cunningham

Till We Have Bodies
Kaalii Cargill, Ph.D.

IMAGES AND STORIES OF MEDUSA have intrigued me since childhood. Every month my mother drove me from the country to visit the Public Library in the city. I browsed the bookshelves to find four books to last me the month. I can still smell the wonderful perfume of old paper and wooden bookshelves. As I searched in the dim light of the old library, I found a shelf marked *Myths and Legends*. The books were arranged in geographical groups, *Myths and Legends of Ancient Greece, Myths and Legends of Scandinavia*, and so on. In these books I found stories that made sense of my world, especially my inner world of feelings and fears, of monsters under the bed, and evil spirits possessing the people I loved. The myths and legends also confirmed my suspicion that Nature was filled with a living presence that could communicate meaning, and that there were forces at work beyond my rational understanding.

The love affair with myth continued in my adult work—I completed a Ph.D. exploring ancient women's mysteries in relation to birth control, and I worked with ritual to reenact ancient myths.

These reenactments involve building sacred space or *temenos* within which women encounter Goddess in Her many forms. One of the forms is what we call "Dark Goddess" although, as we know, there must be light to cast a shadow.

Dark Goddess comes to us in many ways—through emotions, body symptoms, heartbreak, loss, and disappointment. She also comes through our encounters in Nature. On one retreat, as I was sitting in meditation in sacred space in the Australian bush, I opened my eyes to see a huge spider walking straight for me across the floor. It was so big that it was hard to find a jar or bowl large enough to catch it and relocate it to a tree outside. It was very unusual for a spider to be making such determined progress in broad daylight across the open floor in a room full of people. What I later discovered was that the spider was walking directly to the altar set up to honour Dark Goddess. Symbol of Goddess as the spinner and weaver of Fate, the spider knew exactly where it was going.

Over the years, I have learned to respect visits from the Goddess in her creature form, both in dreams and waking encounters. Even when I am uneasy in Her presence, these encounters are opportunities to reconnect with an embodied experience of women's mysteries in the midst of the modern world. We lose a valuable connection if we automatically kill these messengers before paying attention to the authentic emotional and visceral response they have the power to evoke. Encountering Dark Goddess can be very much like coming upon a large spider unexpectedly—Nature providing us with opportunities to feel the presence of Goddess in our lives.

During another ritual retreat, Nature presented me with Goddess in her Medusa form. One of the ritual processes evoked severe constriction in my throat. This cleared through some yelling and crying, releasing fear and rage from my throat. Next morning, in the exact spot where I had been expressing the emotions, there was a Medusa-like cluster of spit-fire caterpillars. These long, black, writhing wasp larvae group together in a remarkable imitation of Medusa's hair and are named for the acidic fluid they spit in defense. They are usually found hanging in trees but, in this case, they were on the ground exactly where I had been sitting the day before.

Spiders and spitting caterpillars—Nature engaging us viscerally, waking us up to the embodied experience of Goddess. It is easy to dismiss these encounters as nothing but strange coincidences—an attempt by the rational, logos function to deny the living relationship with Nature, to deny the manifestation of the extraordinary in the ordinary which is one way Goddess speaks to us. When I have worked with any group of women, there are so many of these meaningful coincidences, from the sublime to the ridiculous, that I am certain this is one way to experience the sacred in the everyday.

Spiders and spitting caterpillars—and snakes. Scary. Dangerous. To be avoided. Very much how contemporary "developed" culture treats strong women and Goddess—scary, dangerous, to be avoided. Yet the strong, instinctual women are still there in stories and images from mythology across cultures and time—in the form of Medusa. She has been known as the Destroyer aspect of the Triple Goddess called Neith in Egypt, Ath-enna or Athene in North Africa[138]. It is through Medusa that mythology offers a hint of what may once have been possible for women in terms of birth control.

Medusa's inscription at Sais called her "mother of all the gods, whom she bore before childbirth existed." [139] The hidden, dangerous face of Medusa is said to have represented Death, which no mortal can see without being turned to stone. Another interpretation is that Medusa was veiled because she was the Future that is hidden from human view. Yet another meaning of her dangerous face was the menstrual taboo.[140] An early work on mythology described how pre-industrial people often believed that the look of a menstruating woman could turn a man to stone.[141] Medusa was understood to have magic blood that could create and destroy life, and that represented the dreaded life and death giving "moon-blood" of women. A female face surrounded by serpent-hair was an ancient, widely recognised symbol of divine feminine

---

[138] BG Walker, 1983, *The Woman's Encyclopaedia of Myths and Secrets,* New York, Harper & Row.
[139] *Larousse Encyclopaedia of Mythology,* 1968, London, Hamlyn Publishing Group, p. 37.
[140] Walker, 1983, op.cit., p. 629.
[141] JG Frazer, 1922, *The Golden Bough,* New York, Macmillan.

wisdom, and equally of the "wise blood" that gave women their powers.

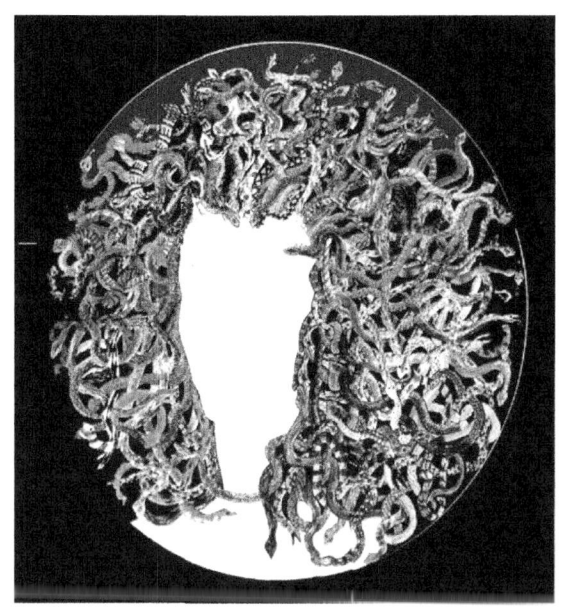

"Medusa"
Original in pencil. Lisa McGuire

If the power of Medusa's wise blood is explored, it becomes obvious that menstrual blood represented the mysterious magic of creation from the earliest of human cultures. It is likely that men developed a superstitious dread for women's monthly bleeding, as they saw the life-blood leave the body without any apparent wounding and no pain, an experience unknown to them.[142] Even the words for menstruation in many early cultures meant things like 'incomprehensible,' 'supernatural,' and 'sacred.' At the time when all Gods were seen to recognise the centrality of the archetypal Great Mother, who manifested as the spirit of creation, Her menstrual blood was central to their power. These are potent descriptions of a time (mythological and/or historical) when "God

---

[142] Walker, op. cit., p. 635.

was a woman," [143] when the prevailing myths told of women's power and mysteries, and when the secrets of fertility resided totally with women.

During trips to Europe, I went looking for images and representations of Goddess, from the magnificent pagan Sibyls in the Sistine Chapel to the stunningly beautiful statue of Artemis of Ephesus. And the Medusa heads—hundreds of Medusa heads but no bodies anywhere. In Florence I came face to face with Caravaggio's painting of Medusa's severed head.

In Istanbul, She is everywhere—even upside down in the ancient Basilica Cistern. In Sicily, Her severed head is a talisman against evil. But where was Her body?

---

[143] M Stone, 1978, *When God Was a Woman,* New York, Harcourt Brace Jovanovich.

I returned home gripped with need to re-member Medusa—to bring together Her head and body. Then I visited the Jean Paul Gaultier fashion exhibition at the National Gallery in Melbourne. The mannequins came to life with projected faces, eyes and lips moving as if real. Ah ha! At last, I knew how to reconnect Medusa's head and body...

I ordered a life-size mannequin online, selecting one that at least looked like a real woman. I ordered three packets of artificial long, black hair. I collected snakeskins and prepared Her clothes...

I expected Her to look powerful and perhaps terrifying at first glance. What I had not expected was for Her to look beautiful. After all, Ovid tells us that the once beautiful Medusa was punished by Athena with a hideous appearance and loathsome snakes for hair because she had been raped in Athena's temple by Poseidon.

Huh? A woman punished and shamed for a man's violence? Why does that sound so familiar? And why had I unconsciously accepted Medusa's hideousness?

As I brought Her present, reconnecting (re-membering) Her head and Her body, I was once again reminded to always look past the patriarchal stories to the truth. Here She is—powerful, terrifying when you catch a glimpse of Her out of the corner of your eye, and so beautiful—Medusa restored.

PS: *The snakeskins are a gift from my Diamond Python—named "Medusa" by my 6-year-old granddaughter.*

Medusa, Athena, Sophia:
the Fierceness of Wisdom Justice

Bonnie Odiorne, AW, Ph.D.

> *"For myself, I have wondered decades ago, would the comprehension of this visage as one of Divine Wisdom—from Monster to Divine Wisdom, change our minds sufficiently so as to affect the way we relate to Earth, to being? I wondered: "What might it mean for our minds to welcome Her back?"*
> —Glenys Livingstone

IMAGINE HER. Her beauty, impassive radiance, intertwines with horror. It captivates with barely glimpsed serpents that slither away to the corners of the eye. We cannot look at her face directly, as the patriarchs could not view Yahweh's. She radiates a power too great for the appropriating gaze. Perseus used her reflection on Athena's shield to sever her head; she is glimpsed through a mirror, brilliantly.

French feminist critical theorists have discussed how the feminine subverts the certainties that patriarchy uses to dominate and appropriate woman. Medusa, by becoming monstrous, both escapes the patriarchal gaze and subverts it. Luce Irigarry, in *Speculum de l'autre: Femme,* traces how the reflection in the mirror—speculum, speculation—of the woman as Other, distorts the certainties of language, political and moral values and hierarchies. Hélène Cixous writes with a language that exuberantly celebrates Medusa laughing, **and** insidiously inserts desire and the body where they do not 'belong.'

Medusa is transformed, dis-figured, for flaunting her beauty before the Goddess Aphrodite, who recognizes no rivals. This is Aphrodite as Dark Goddess, combining the political and the erotic (Menee 2017). Thus, the dark side of the goddess of Love sets Medusa, as

Livingstone argues, on her journey to Wisdom. Monstrous, Medusa slips within and around language, escapes words that seek to petrify categories into ossified reality that we think we can possess, control, and appropriate. She personifies feminine eroticism and energy. She belongs to no one: not to Perseus who beheaded her and had thought to vanquish her by bringing her head to Athena. She does not even belong to Athena, Goddess of Wisdom and War, Goddess of the city and civilized life, who appears to be an archetype of divine feminine self-sufficiency and mastery. Wisdom/Athena as artisan invented objects and processes that allowed civilization to develop—the subjugation of the earth through cities and agriculture: the bit that tamed horses, allowing them to go to war, the yoke for oxen, the plough. She also invented the earthenware pot for cooking, and storing, spinning, weaving—as well as musical instruments. Athena defended the city, and embodied war, carried a shield and spear. Her birth from the head of Zeus erased any previous feminine origins (a Titaness who also represented Wisdom). She is a virgin goddess and belongs to no man. Nevertheless, Zeus amplifies Athena's power and grants her his shield and Aegis. There She places Medusa's head, seemingly superfluous to the power of the god Medusa, representing that which civilization cannot appropriate even as it attempts to, reinforces and subverts the combined power of goddess and god. Athena's aegis with Medusa's head paralyzes with Beauty and Horror. Athena as War goddess vanquishes, defends the city, civilization. She embodies humankind's domination of the earth. What does Wisdom represent? Athena creates much that civilizes but She also dominates: she is also, as Medusa is, impassive, grey-eyed. As Livingstone argues, Medusa journeys from human beauty to a personification of a sun Goddess (her serpent hair its wavy rays) whom no one can gaze upon. Her journey ends with Wisdom. She is visibly present with the Goddess, and projects Warrior Wisdom's attributes. Do Wisdom/Athena and Medusa integrate, or do they rather represent what cannot be 'mastered?'—another way of relating to the world: the earth in a mode (other than that of exploitation, extraction, theft that in turn dominates other humans.)

I suggest a rapid transit from Greek mythology to pre-common era Jewish Alexandria to find another view of Wisdom. The Wisdom (Hebrew: *Hochmah*) tradition that was present throughout the Hebrew scriptures is Grecianized (Greek: *Sophia*, as in *philo sophia*, love of wisdom, philosophy) to better reflect Alexandrian culture. Sophia, Wisdom, found most obviously in Proverbs, is beauty, treasure and gentle delight to those who embrace her and cling to Her fiercely. She is also, as is Athena, artisan, present with Yahweh at creation. Sophia in Proverbs is also a warrior and fights for those whom the Wicked, the powerful, oppress, who drain life from that which belongs to all: the virtues of the *demos,* the Commons. While Athena protects and defends, represents the city, Sophia calls out to the city, admonishes the foolish to listen and understand, accept Her invitation to the house she has built for Herself and humanity. She offers mutuality, abundance, a banquet with wine… to the Wicked who offer only domination of the powerless.

> "Is not Wisdom calling?… she takes her stand by the gates, at the entrance to the city, on the access roads, she cries out, 'I am calling to you, **all people**, my words are addressed to **all humanity**.'" Prov. 8:1-4 (Jerusalem, emphasis mine)

Bruce Sanguin in "Walking With Wisdom" describes a path that is everything good and beautiful, but "it shall be just, for She is outraged by oppression of all her children" (*If Darwin Prayed,* Kindle 2680). *This* is the Wisdom who stands in the marketplace, on the heights of the city, at its crossroads, its access roads and cries out to **all** to become acquainted with Her ways. Her call is sweetness and enticement, but also close to the wildness of nature. (Athena has the impassive owl, night huntress, as her avatar.) Sophia rages at the pain and suffering brought by the foolish, the unjust, who do not listen. Hers is a fierce hospitality offered as a warning: If humans reject Her abundance, they will be judged harshly in the unyielding dichotomy of Proverbs. Good/evil, wise/foolish, righteous/wicked. She burns brightly, yet is veiled from "ordinary" perception—else why would so many not have heard her call? She is the dark mother whom patriarchy cannot banish (Rhiannon). Wisdom is offended by injustice. Her voice is strong. If we are called to walk her path, we must be equally forceful in sharing Her message of justice for all humankind and the world that is our home.

> "She makes you a beacon for goodness and fairness.
> She will not protect you from trouble,
> but makes you troublesome
> to those who seek to advance on the backs of others."
> (Montfort, Shapiro, 100, 22)

What does Wisdom Sophia do? She shines the beacon of justice ("goodness and fairness") and illuminates injustice ("those who seek to advance on the back of others"); her fire is incandescent. She also projects the power of the Medusa. She offers love, beauty and delight, but those who wish to follow Her are not safe from harm. They are compelled to act, and She makes them troublemakers. She is trouble, particularly for those who practice injustice for their own advantage. Her light is unforgiving, harsh upon the unjust with power. She does not allow them to take it for granted. Wisdom (Athena and Sophia) as beauty and goodness combine with Medusa's beautiful power and questions, calls, harasses, creates trouble and troublemakers. That which is perceived as monstrous has a power that cannot be silenced, or unseen. With Wisdom Sophia, Medusa's visage is transformed. She becomes the face of all those who are marginalized, oppressed, excluded, who demand a place on the earth.

Interestingly, King Solomon, prays to 'possess' Sophia, as the patriarchy models, and God grants her *and* wealth to him. Solomon (1 Kings 3) seems to foreshadow the prophecy of Isaiah, the embodiment of the just ruler. The passage can just as easily refer to Jesus, Wisdom incarnate, advocate for justice, Wisdom teacher:

> "The spirit of the Lord shall rest upon him, the spirit of

wisdom and understanding, the spirit of counsel and might, he will know the Lord's will and honor him and find pleasure in obeying Him. He will not judge by appearance or hearsay, he will judge the poor fairly and defend the rights of the helpless." (Is 11:2-4)

It is telling, and tragically ironic, that it is Solomon's prayer from the *Book of Wisdom* that Cardinal Timothy Michael Dolan quoted to begin the inauguration of Donald Trump. Wisdom is a desirable quality in a new president, if this had been a normal transition. Yet we cannot imagine a president least likely to ask for Wisdom in governance:

"God of our ancestors and Lord of mercy, you have made all things. And in your providence have charged us to rule the creatures produced by you, to govern the world in holiness and righteousness, and to render judgment with integrity of heart. Give us wisdom, for we are your servants, weak and short-lived, lacking in comprehension of judgment and of laws. Indeed, though one might be perfect among mortals, if wisdom which comes from you be lacking, we count for nothing. Now with you is wisdom, who knows your will and was there when you made the world, who understands what is pleasing in your eyes, what is conformable with your commands, send her forth from your holy heavens. From your glorious throne, dispatch her that she may be with us and work with us, that we may grasp what is pleasing to you. For she knows and understands all things and will guide us prudently in our affairs and safeguard us by her glory." (1 Kings 3, Wisdom 9:9-17, CNN)

Protestants, largely represented at the Inauguration by the evangelical right, do not recognize the *Book of Wisdom* as part of canonical scripture: written much later, this book is part of the 'Apocrypha.' (Evangelicals might have recognized the 1 Kings 3 passage). The "her" might have disrupted those who paid attention, who listened. They could thus without guilt ignore the warning implicit in the passage quoted to inaugurate the 'coronation' of an authoritarian ruler chosen by God.

Wisdom, 'veiled Sophia,' has a forceful dark side that underlies the (feminine) resistance. The administration's dark side aligns more with the Éminence grise (Saturday Night Live portrayed 'President Bannon' as Death). Mr. Bannon has unrepentantly admitted to channeling Darth Vader. As a counter to unquestioned rule untempered by "holiness and righteousness... integrity of heart," the Women's March exploded forcefully, surpassed all expectations. Inevitably compared to the (under-attended) inauguration, it wounded the president's pretense of power and his fragile ego. Images of woman power included the late Carrie Fisher as Princess Leia that flourished on Internet memes resisting Darth Vader:

> A woman's place is in the Resistance
> A million voices cried out. Don't be silent now.
> Fuck this imperialist bullshit
> ...Take note, Skywalker boys. Y'all weak as shit.

Medusa's journey to Wisdom enlarges one woman's story and expands it to the world. She reinforces Athena's power yet subverts it as simple domination: as war, as civilization mastering the earth. With Sophia she extends to injustice, such as what she herself experienced from a powerful, vain and capricious goddess. Medusa figuratively transfers to Sophia, whose fierce light illuminates injustice as her voice calls it out. I like to think that Medusa/Sophia/Dark Mother is at work within and in opposition to the current administration and the resistance. Stephen Bannon, the president and a colluding Republican congress think to tame her and inflict ever greater abuses of power—a modern Perseus. We know the fate of those who purport to gaze upon her. Petrified.

REFERENCES:

Cixous, H. Keith Cohen; Paula Cohen, tr. *Signs*, Vol. 1, No. 4. (Summer, 1976), pp. 875-893.

CNN "Presidential Inauguration Begins with King Solomon's Prayer" Politics January 20, 2017.

Irigarry, L. *Speculum de l'autre: Femme.* Paris: Éditions du seuil, 1974.

Livingstone G. "Medusa: Sister, Mother, Mirror, Abyss." April 7, 2016.

Meenee, H. "Fighting Fascists in the Streets of Athens." Posted on January 30, 2017 by RTM Admin Editor Goddesses.

Rhyannon, "Dark matrix, dark matter, dark mother." Jan. 11, 2017, Mago Works.

Sanguin, B. *If Darwin Prayed. Prayers for Evolutionary Mystics.* Vancouver, BC, Canada: Vancouver Desktop Publishing Centre. Kindle. 2010.

Shapiro, R. *The Love of Eternal Wisdom: A Revisioning of Saint Louis De Montfort's Contemplation on Divine Wisdom.* Litchfield, CT: Wisdom House. 2012.

Black Medusa
Cristina Biaggi, Ph.D.

The Black Medusa is a sculpture of my face many years ago with collages of women looking at the viewer, some well-known. She has a sardonic look on her face as many Medusas do. The Black Medusa is 3 and one half feet in diameter.

Red Medusa
Cristina Biaggi, Ph.D.

The Red Medusa, or the Laughing Medusa, is a sculpture of my daughter. Laughter is a political tool. "She who laughs, lasts." (I had a bumper sticker saying that.) Surrounding the Red Medusa are women laughing, some uproariously while looking at the viewer. Just like the Black Medusa, the Red one is a collage and sculpture on a wood background. The Red Medusa is 5 feet in diameter.

Marija K.
Jack K. Jeansonne

Those Who Do Not Fear
Marija Krstic

I see the idea of Medusa as a woman having visible images representing her passion dancing around her head. These dancing images imply independent and abundant creative expression, which can appear scary and ugly to those who feel threatened by a strong, confident, evolved woman and by witnessing unapologetic manifestations of her thoughts, intentions, potential and timeless connection to creative source. The fearful are "turned to stone" or stunned and confused by an image that contradicts their limited and limiting beliefs and their training, since infancy, about what a woman's limitations and acceptable behaviors ought to be. Those who do not fear should feel empowered and join in a celebration of passion and creative freedom while finding their own inner-Medusa.

For me, this Medusa image represents feminine power and mystery. The guitar necks, as part of the head, show a direct way of communicating thoughts and emotions through the magic of music.

Medusa's Hairdresser
Penny-Anne Beaudoin

the serpentine look was my idea
a work of art if i do say so
i call it 'hiss'

every saturday
i give her a wash and set
a mani and a pedi
and hear her confession
offer her reflection a sympathetic glance or two
cluck and tut in all the right places

why do they look? she cries

i don't know, honey, i just don't know

it's like they can't help themselves
they know they shouldn't
but they do
every time
every damn time

that's a fact sweetie, every single damn time

they peek and peep and ogle and stare
between   the curtains
                the pages
                the sheets
online
offline
        down blouses
        up skirts

        in theatres
        strip joints
        change rooms
        health clubs for god's sake

oh it's a shame, is what it is, a cryin' shame
they look and look
and feel themselves grow hard
    but from the inside out, you know?
    from the heart out in all directions

that they do, baby, that they do

feel themselves grow stone cold hard
until they can't feel anything anymore

uh-uh, not a thing, not one blessed thing

like they're dead

um-hm, dead dead dead

like they kill themselves
and die
with their eyes wide open

that's right baby, wide wide open

Medusa
Susan Hawthorne

Photo taken at an exhibition held in the Museo Massimo,
Rome in early 2014.

Medusa, My Mother and Me

Barbara C. Daughter

AS A TEENAGER IN THE LATE 1940s, my mother attended Girls' Latin, a prestigious public school in Boston. The school's focus on a Western Classical preparatory curriculum doubtlessly included Greek mythology, which was one possible source of her information about Medusa. It was likely she saw paintings or sculpture of her at the Museum of Fine Arts—or possibly that her parents' and other relatives' interests in literature and the arts contributed to her understanding of the snake-headed woman of antiquity. Naturally, her knowledge of and understanding of the world, and the ages before her, were shaped by the culture in which she lived: patriarchy before the second wave of feminism in the United States. For her, holding a positive view of the beheaded icon was improbable.

Fast forward some twenty years. Up to this point in my life, I do not specifically recall Mom mentioning the gods and goddesses of Greek mythology. However, I remember clearly the derision and disdain in her voice, devoid of any respect or awe, when she declared, upon seeing my second-grade school photo, "You look like Medusa!" Picture, if you will, a nervous eight-year old girl whose blonde hair has been futilely coaxed into banana curls. On her nose are perched new, slightly askew, sparkly blue cat's-eye glasses. How could I, at this innocent age and awkward time in my life, resemble the fearsome Medusa?

Ever since that fateful comment, Medusa has intrigued and haunted me. While I do not remember the original photo—Mom ensured it was re-taken—I vividly recall the second version of the photo in which my hair was tamer, but I still looked like the anxious youngster I was. But maybe it was not my stringy hair that she was repelled by; perhaps my eyes had Medusa's look of sheer terror. Was it my snake-like hair, or my pupils widened with fear, that reminded my mother of Medusa? To this day, in many photographs my eyes still belie my unease.

I am certain I asked her who Medusa was, and while I was given an explanation, I do not remember seeing an image of her at the time. In contrast, on one of my school field trips to a Boston museum, I memorized and became entranced with a replica of the small statue Arthur Evans is said to have unearthed at Knossos, Crete, Greece: the Minoan Snake Goddess. Imaginably, I unknowingly conflated the two. Who were these snake-wielding women and what could they reveal to me? Was Medusa my nemesis, as my mother's tone implied, to be feared and avoided? Or a secret source of wonder and inspiration, a hidden treasure I could draw upon for reassurance? Could she model a different way of being in the world?

This was the same year that my mother commented on my "difference" from others... to what was she referring? *"Why do you have to be so different?"* she lamented. I was completely baffled by this comment, yet on some instinctual level knew it was true, but not "how." Was it my inherent inability to "go along to get along," or to think the same way as others, and still speak my mind? As a second-grader, how could I understand this comment, and more importantly, know what she wanted me to do and be instead?

Who was Medusa to my mother? Certainly a fearsome, ugly woman. As a girl, my mother had been called "the smart one," while her developmentally-delayed sister, about a year older, was called, "the pretty one." While my grandparents' comments may have been well-intended, calling out the best attributes of each of their daughters, their remarks led to a pronounced lack of self-esteem for my mother. Is it any wonder she wished for her own child to be seen as attractive?

Second grade seems to be a time of physical transformation for many youngsters. The bright-eyed, plump-cheeked children of first grade yield to lankier bodies and adult teeth in eight-year-old's mouths, an often awkward combination. As they mature, second graders experience reinforced social norms and greater expectations for appropriate behavior and appearances. For me, these changes and my mother's comments led to less confidence in relating to my peers, in school and in my neighborhood. However, while I was not the most popular child, I was nevertheless not dissuaded from speaking up and sharing my own views. What inspired this outspokenness?

Who was Medusa to my mother? I doubt she had read the myth of Athena punishing the *beautiful* Medusa for Poseidon's rape of Medusa in Athena's temple, for if she had, would she not have identified with Medusa's victimization, instead of that of her tormentors? Instead, Mom seemed to regard Medusa as a baneful shrew who stood in stark contrast to our culture's expectations of girls (and women) to be pretty and nice. Medusa was to be feared, but not for her fierceness, but for how far she had fallen from the realm of respectability. The lyrics from Sweet Honey In the Rock's song, "Joan Little," come to mind:

> *"I've always been told since the day I was born, leave those no-good women alone."*

No explicit message was needed: no girl or woman would want to be like Medusa.

Was it any consolation to my mother that in high school I was encouraged to enter the local beauty pageant, a spectacle and opportunity to which she had never been given access? Did she feel any reconciliation or satisfaction that her daughter was not excluded from the ranks of the "pretty" ones?

Even before college, as I began to think more critically about the faith in which I was raised, I questioned the role of women in my church, and why it was restricted to assisting others, rather than positions of direct authority. I chose not to even apply to a Lutheran college I visited that suggested my interest in becoming a counseling pastor would be best served through their deaconess program. Once in college, having begun that inquiry into women's roles in the church, I pursued it further by learning about faith traditions other than the one in which I was raised. While most of these were nevertheless patriarchal traditions, I discovered there were different ways of discerning and naming the Divine than the Judeo-Christian ones I knew about.

When I had the privilege of studying in Cambridge, England, we took advantage of our Eurail passes during spring break to reach a warmer clime; Greece was calling to us. So captivated was I by the stark beauty of the cliffs of Paleokastritsa, stretching to the sparkling Mediterranean Sea below that I fully contemplated not returning to the US. If I had I seen Medusa's likeness at the Temple of Artemis there on the island of Corfu (Kerkyra), would I have felt protected, or just revulsion at her terrible visage?[144] I would not have thought then how her tongue sticking out recalls the fierce Kali. Or with her eyes bulging and her tongue thrust out, how she resembles the Maori as they perform the Haka, a war challenge/dance.

Next, I traveled to Athens, where I bought an intricate charm of Athena which for years after, I wore daily. On it, one can see traces of Medusa's face on Athena's shield. What would I have thought if I had known then that her image was emblazoned across the shield of Athena? As I derived inspiration from Athena's warrior-like reputation, how much of that should I have ascribed to Medusa's protection?

Sometime during my college years or shortly thereafter, my mother purchased a postcard of the Minoan Snake Goddess and tacked it on the kitchen bulletin board. Did she not see the possible relationship between her and Medusa? As a Lutheran, in a heavily Catholic community, she has shared with me her beliefs about not idolizing saints or even the Virgin Mary. What compelled her to buy this image, she has never revealed. Try as I might, I could not convince her to part with it, despite my exhortations that I had first

---

[144] See page 38.

seen this figurine as a child at the museum, was mesmerized with her even then, and now as a pagan adult was actively seeking images of the Divine in female form.

Decades later, journeying with Carol Christ on a Goddess Pilgrimage to Crete, I had the opportunity to see the two statuettes of these snake-wielding women—were they Goddesses?—at the Heraklion Museum. Traversing the steps at Knossos, Kato Zakros, and other ancient sites, the stones seemed to pull from my feet a rhythm, a retracing of a familiar dance, perhaps. I felt I could lay my cheek on the smooth stone benches and somehow be comfortable, on a cellular level, in this land that once knew women who were unafraid to partner with the power and beauty of snakes. As I scoured the shops for souvenirs, I looked for a charm of the Minoan Snake Woman, similar to the one I had of Athena, but was disappointed to find so many had the look of terror in her eyes, reminiscent of Medusa's gaze. Eyes widened so that one can see the sclera above and/or below the iris is known by the Japanese as "*sanpuku*," a condition which demonstrates a lack of physical, mental and/or spiritual stability. How did the ancient Minoans perceive this gaze? Was she in a state of ecstasy? Or was she also terrified?

Throughout my abundant travels that year, I would continue to find and be captivated by ancient images of powerful women with snakes. In St. Petersburg, Russia at the Hermitage Museum, I longed to get closer to the mosaic of Medusa cordoned off from visitors. If she was such a loathsome creature, as I had been led to believe, why was her image replicated in painstaking detail, and imported to such far-flung locations?

While in the Baltic Sea area, I decided to make my own pilgrimage to the homeland of my Motherline; my mother's mother's mother immigrated to the US from Visby, Gotland, Sweden. I stayed in the medieval walled city, fortified from potential attacks not from pirates, but farmers and landholders. At the Gotland Museum, I found my own ancestral connection to these snake-wielding women: a nearly three-feet tall block of stone carved with an image of a woman in a Sheila-na-gig position—while brandishing a snake in each hand—known as the Snake-witch stone, or the Smiss stone. I observed she was an anomaly among the many similarly-carved stones: she is the only one that prominently features a woman without the presence of men. Was there a connection between the Snake-witch and the Minoan Snake Goddess, as some have asserted? Did she also then have a connection to Medusa? Must we regard these snake-connected women as unique only to their own culture? The triskelion motif centered above the Snake-witch, as well as the border detail surrounding the stone, recall Celtic influences. Likewise, could the mythology of the Mediterranean have been imported to the Baltic? Or did dissimilar myths about snake-wielding women exist in these cultures, uninfluenced by the other?

Recently, I tried painting Medusa's image, to understand my experiences with her. *She stares at me, haunted and haunting from the canvas. Of what is she terrified, this alleged muse of mine? I called out for her to reveal herself, to guide me. Expecting to be assuaged instead I am confronted. Her fear, mine.*

Last year, while visiting my family in Boston, we planned a trip to one of my favorite museums: the Isabella Stewart Gardner Museum. Accompanied by my enthusiastic Mom and somewhat reluctant Dad, we sauntered through the Venetian-style, white marble palace. There in the open courtyard, who should we find? Staring back from her imported, centuries-old mosaic, Medusa reminded me: she is yet fierce, frightened and enigmatic.

My Name is Medusa
Arna Baartz

Early sketch for the *My Name is Medusa* children's book by Glenys Livingstone Ph.D.

Medusa Goddess: Up Close and Personal
Marie Summerwood

THE FIRST TIME I knowingly met the presence of Medusa, I was being initiated as a priestess. My lover and I planned the ritual ourselves, or so we thought. It was in the middle of the night during winter solstice, the deepest darkest time of winter. We had rented a cabin in the woods, snowy, silent and still. The intention was deep. We went to sleep early and set a small sweet bell alarm in the other room that would awaken us as though we were being called by the [imagined] sisters of our temple. Our bedside altar held candles, ritual objects and a small feast for afterward. I had planned to call upon several goddesses to stand with me in various aspects of my power: Isis would be called to help me remember I am a sacred woman; Quan Yin for the strength of my joy and my ability to sing out in the sacred power of grief; and of course, Mary—my namesake—She who is present at the doorway of life and death in my world and holds me in Her sacred heart, always. And I had planned to call upon Aphrodite to come and stand with me in the name of Beauty, which I ultimately was free to do, but not before another goddess showed up.

A note here. My strategy, in addressing a goddess energy that I want to work with, is to ultimately promise Her that I will tell Her story. And I do, with my teaching and my chants. Especially my chants. To keep the goddesses alive and strong in our hearts, we tell Their stories, sing about Them—and Their powers. It works. They love it.

Anyway, we awoke to the temple bells and began. It was a simple yet deep ritual, and one of important surrender. We cast the circle and chanted. I called Isis and smiled, I invoked Quan Yin and felt at ease. Mary brought me home to my own sacred heart. At the moment though, the moment when I had planned to speak the name of the next goddess, my hands clenched and unclenched and

I found myself fiercely whispering—over and over—the name of Medusa. It went on for several long moments. From my astonished depths I felt her name rise in me as I heard my own voice say, "I will tell your story, Medusa, I will tell Your Story." So here I am.

According to Edith Hamilton, Medusa is one of the Gorgons, a trio of evil sisters who share one eye. She is the only mortal one of the sisters and is so ugly and fearsome that she has snakes for hair. So fearsome and ugly that She is deadly to behold; and one look into Her eyes turns men to stone. After Perseus slew Her, the blood dripping from Her severed head gave birth to the wingèd horse, Pegasus, and to legions of demons. That is some powerful blood.

For years, this story of Medusa was my only source of information. My oppression was still in place, and I could not yet imagine there might even be other versions of Medusa's story—perhaps a version where Medusa is a serpent-goddess of the Libyan Amazons, descended from Lamia, the Libyan serpent goddess of creation? Or one where Medusa is the Crone/Destroyer aspect of Neith, The Triple Goddess in Egypt? Or perhaps one where our re-claimed, re-found, re-sung goddess Medusa shows up when we pray or chant to Her (and where She has our back!) as we stand in our own authentic fierceness. Her name, Medusa, comes from linguistic roots meaning "female wisdom." Gorgon masks were used by more than one culture; the women wore them in ritual. A woman's face surrounded by serpent hair is an ancient symbol worn by those whose work it is to protect blood mysteries and divine female wisdom.

No small wonder then, that in the twisted creation story of the next religion—Christianity—an evil snake gets a woman in trouble over knowledge SHE is not supposed to have.

In Edith's Classical Greek story, Perseus beheads Medusa and brings her head to Athena, who wears it forevermore on Her breastplate.

The real King Perseus (circa 1209 B.C.E.) and his armies fought against and slaughtered the Amazons and other peoples of the matrifocal cultures. The Greek story was rewritten to indicate that Medusa, the divine female wisdom, has been destroyed and is now relegated to mere ornamentation. The mythology of the people was changed, and over time their basic beliefs were affected, but not lost.

For me—in that deep ritual and visitation—for us as women of power, it was and is clearly time to fully reclaim Medusa as a Goddess of protection and fierceness! Fierce means "Wild and Proud." Fierce as the Mother Bear; fierce as the old woman, the crone, the giver of death; fierce as the Amazons who stood in sacred circle to fall together.

In my own ritual work with the energies of the directions I feel a spectrum of emotional stories in each. Medusa appears in the South. For me the South holds the vibrations of Passion, of Anger, Outrage, Rage, and anything in between—including Enthusiasm, Fierceness, Eagerness and Zealotry. When I call Her, Medusa comes, and She comes in fierceness instead of deadly danger. She brings wild pride instead of rage, untamed beauty instead of armor. We can heal from the frozen night desert of rage with Her at our back. Medusa holds the place of rage as a sacred power of the women together. Medusa offers us Her shield of fierceness whenever we need it. Medusa helps us come forward into the world in our own untamed beauty, in our own passionate fierceness. Medusa is shielded in the power of Her own fierce beauty. May every woman's face be engraved upon the shield of Medusa. I know mine is.

I chant to open to Her fierceness,
I chant to remember my own truth about Medusa.
Let us chant to Her:
Ave Medusa
Fierce woman wild and proud, stand in the gaze of Medusa!
Fierce woman wild and proud, stand in the gaze of Medusa!
Sacred daughter of Her, sacred daughter of Her
My face adorns the shield of Medusa.
Sacred daughter of Her, sacred daughter of Her
My face adorns the shield of Medusa.
Ave Medusa, Ave Medusa, Ave Medusa, Ave Medusa!

From the CD, "Step Into The River" © 2006 by Marie Summerwood msummerw@twcny.rr.com

Sicilian Tambourine
Susan Hawthorne

Photo of a tambourine purchased in Sicily.

Baubo
Susan Hawthorne

the hours of talk were long
and they have agreement

Baubo is leading a morning ritual
she is flanked by Demeter and Medusa
it begins as a low belly rumble
releases into a wide open laugh

laughter ricochets around the circle
infecting each one of us
Baubo makes Demeter laugh again
Medusa laughs her head off

La Befana is running around
with her other half Perchta
handing out honeyed figs and dates

their broomsticks are for
sweeping the sky
not sweeping floors

we laugh at our pain
we laugh to stay sane

This was first published in Susan's book, *Lupa and Lamb*, Spinifex Press, 2014.

Medusa's Hall of Mirrors
Leslene della-Madre

THE GODDESS MEDUSA is often saddled with a menacing, hideous and threatening reputation, and like the Hindu Kali, falls into the so-called "terrible aspect" of the Goddess. With hissing snakes for hair and an "evil eye" stare, she incited a cold fear in those who gazed upon her and turned them to stone. In the Classical Greek myth of the Gorgon sisters, she is the crone aspect or devouring aspect of what novelist and poet Robert Graves called the Triple Moon Goddess. In some patriarchal variations of the myth, the three sisters were all thought to be "monsters" described as:

> ...girded with serpents, vibrating tongues, gnashing their teeth, having wings, brazen claws, and enormous teeth. In later myths (mainly in Ovid) Medusa was the only Gorgon to possess snake locks, because they were a punishment from Athena. Accordingly, Ovid relates that the once beautiful mortal was punished by Athena with a hideous appearance and loathsome snakes for hair for having been raped in Athena's temple by Poseidon.[145]

She also hails origins from Libya in North Africa, preceding the Greeks where she was known as Neith—who was also found in the Egyptian pantheon. The Egyptians said her name means "I have come from myself"[146] which to me is a whisper across the expanse of time beckoning a remembrance of the ancient parthenogenetic Goddess. To know the goddess Neith was to know death, as the inscription on her temple at Sais reads, "I am all that has been, that will be, and no mortal has yet been able to lift the veil that covers me," for to see her was to have crossed over from this life.[147]

---

[145] Garcia, http://www.ancient.eu/Medusa/ Ancient History Encyclopedia.
[146] Walker, *Women's Encyclopedia of Myths and Secrets,* p. 721.
[147] George, *Mysteries of the Dark Moon*, p. 155.

Medusa was revered and exalted by the Libyan Amazons as the Queen Serpent Goddess of female wisdom. I think all the ramifications of the meaning of this title remain mysterious because female wisdom is denied in patriarchy and women must search beneath the hardened layers of conditioning to find our true heritage. The most common story of Medusa, whose name from ancient Greek *medo* means "to protect, to rule over"[148] and "the ruling one,"[149] tells the aggrandized patriarchal tale of jealousy, betrayal, rape and murder. In this myth the goddess is split into her "good" and "bad" aspects forcing her to appear to fight against herself—Athena, the daughter born from the forehead of her father, created in alignment with patriarchy as the male myth makers wished, and Medusa, the mortal Gorgon who was punished by Athena. The goddess punishes herself—a very strange, confused and twisted story indeed.

The Classical Greek myths are all variations on these same themes. Demonizing the creative female powers of the cosmos became a high priority for the male-dominated violent hierarchy that sought to replace the more peaceful woman-centered cultures of the Neolithic. In the above-mentioned variation she is blamed for Poseidon raping her, the burden of which still plays out very commonly today, not only in the shame women feel when men rape them but also in the persistent blame that it is a woman's fault if a man rapes her. Classical Greek mythology is the embodiment of both rape culture and a deep-seated misogyny that are the bedrock of Western civilization. I believe that the challenge in dealing with these violent woman-hating mythologies is to learn what lies at the core of these anti-woman and anti-life myths, for the Medusa Archimage[150] is also cross-cultural.

---

[148] http://www.behindthename.com/name/medusa
[149] Dexter, in *Journal of Studies of Feminist Religion*, p. 25
[150] I am using the word "Archimage" from Mary Daly instead of "archetype" because according to Daly, Archimage is a "Metaphoric form of Naming the one and the many. She is power/powers of being within women and all biophilic creatures… She is shimmering Substance—Real Presence—that shines through

In my experience as an independent scholar, writer, shamanic explorer and practitioner and teacher of women's mysteries, I have felt that helping women to reclaim Medusa by symbolically reattaching her head through ritual is deeply empowering. Restoring Medusa's power for women restores sovereign female power, which is the very essence of healing for women in patriarchy. Women living within a patriarchal culture are held in a constant ideation of weakness and inferiority and are seen as sexual objects within the patriarchal pornographic culture, which is a heinous degradation of the more peaceful preceding woman-centered cultures marked by sacred expressions of the beauty of life and cosmos across millennia, seen in the numerous artifacts unearthed by renown archeologists and linguist and archeomythologist Marija Gimbutas. The beheaded Medusa living in the female psyche is a debilitating, fragmented image affecting women in numerous ways. And the fact that a male warrior is heralded as a hero for beheading her has many connotations, most of which lie deep within the unconscious. I feel one of the most obvious manifestations of this violent dynamic can be seen today in the terrible acid maiming of women in India committed by angry men who don't get what they want from women, disfiguring their beauty (not just physical, but inside as well as outside) and causing them great harm, as if it is their right to do so. If the women live through the horror the men inflict on them, their faces become a mask covering the beauty they once knew. If they don't live, they have essentially been beheaded and erased.

Much has been written about the Medusa Archimage from many angles, such as feminism and psychoanalysis. Since psychoanalysis

---

appearances. She is root of connectedness in the female Elemental Race." (*Pure Lust*, p.87) Daly dismantles the word archetype and says, "'Thus it is said to mean 'the original model, from, or pattern from which something is made or from which something develops'... The fact is, that which is truly original cannot be reduced to a model, form, or pattern without serious distortion. For one who is Original is a verb, always be-ing, changing. It is inherent in archetypes that they crush this biophilic lust for being." (*Pure Lust*, p.79) is a field created by men who I feel really did not know anything meaningful about the female psyche, I feel that men like Freud, for instance, actually created a field of study based on male projections, believing that what they thought about women was the gospel truth. The problem of course with this male world was that they were able to exercise great power over women, crowning Freud as the godfather of psychological malethink who had the answers for women as if they had none for themselves—a different kind of beheading. One of the most obvious Freudian projections was his notion that Medusa represented the toothed vagina. Freud was extremely enmeshed with his mother and refused to face his own issues with her. So, my analysis of Freud is that a convoluted projection such as this one was his way of trying to separate from his mother and in order to do so he had to see female genitals as Medusa-like—scary and both castrated and castrating. To Freud, the penis was the sword of power in his world; castrated female genitalia implied a loss of power and the castrating female genitalia implied a taking of power. I think Freud felt castrated by his mother but could not face his own unconscious. So, he made a big fat theory about it and projected it onto women. In my view, his theory said women were envious of the male penis and felt castrated; if they couldn't have one of their own, they would clamp down on it in sexual intercourse and steal it, thereby acting out castration. I know. Weird. If any woman came up with a rival theory about men such as this she would have been laughed out of existence or locked up. But Freud's fear of the powerful female rendered him unable to understand his own wounding.

The female genitalia were also seen as a wound by men of his time—a vision that rendered women weak and in need of perpetual healing in men's eyes. Of course, then the good doctor and his cohorts could come to their heroic rescue.[151] Another esteemed male definer of women's reality and colleague of Freud,

---

[151] A wound not in the same sense as the "wise wound" as written about by Penelope Shuttle and Peter Redgrove in the book *The Wise Wound*.

Karl Abraham, agreed with him and wrote in his essay *The Female Castration Complex*, "The female genital is looked upon as a wound, and as such it represents an effect of castration"[152] as if the human default is male, which is, of course, a reversal of truth. The creation of male psychoanalysis of the female has filled volumes of not only what men thought about womens' psychological status but also what they thought they should do for, about and to women, all of which is beyond the scope of this article. Suffice it to say that this mirror in Medusa's hall of mirrors reflects a grim and distorted view of women and our bodies revealing how the men behind the mirror, like the Wizard of Oz, were devoid of real love and in fact, while trembling in fear, did not know who Medusa really was.

Another mirror in her hallway is the one that reflects to women our real power. Medusa as the third face in the Triple Moon Goddess is the crone—she who understands the secrets of life, death and transformation. Some feminist scholars feel the Triple Goddess is a recent invention created by Robert Graves. While she might be, the truth and energy behind the face of Medusa is timeless and can be recognized as a woman's true sovereign power of self-knowledge. Some feminist writers think that Medusa represents the pent-up rage of women being forced to live as second-class citizens, regarded as tokens and playthings and enslaved in a man's world as objects men can rape whenever they please, as we find in the Classical Greek myths. What woman wouldn't have rage at such a reality? In 1971, the Unitarian Universalist poet May Sarton wrote a poem titled "The Muse as Medusa," in which she explores the power of Medusa as a source of inspiration:

> I saw you once, Medusa; we were alone.
> I looked you straight in the cold eye, cold.
> I was not punished, was not turned to stone.
> How to believe the legends I am told? …

---

[152] Abraham, *Selected Papers of Karl Abraham,* p. 340.

I turned your face around! It is my face.
That frozen rage is what I must explore —
Oh secret, self-enclosed, and ravaged place!
That is the gift I thank Medusa for.[153]

The late Ann Scales—feminist, lawyer, activist and law professor—regarded Medusa as a relevant and potent force that men cannot do away with no matter how hard they might try. She says that Medusa is dangerous because:

> By turning men to stone, she prevented "the male gaze," thus denying the possibility that women could be defined by men... Her snakes represent unintimidatable self-possession. She had to be killed because, by her very existence, she could expose the contingency of the Law of the Fathers... Medusa symbolizes female *potential*.
>
> In short, Medusa is the unvarnished, undomesticated... counternarrative to patriarchy.[154]

Scales introduces a profound naming she termed "scarring the sacred" that describes what men have done to Nature, as in defacing the Black Hills at Mt. Rushmore with the egotistical rendering of the faces of male presidents as if they were more potent than the hills themselves, as an attempt to achieve immortality—the Perseus pursuit. She points out this male obsession can be seen in the early myth of Gilgamesh who desecrates the sacred forest, and of course in Perseus' assault on Medusa. Her brilliant idea that Medusa is the counternarrative to patriarchy gives women permission to stand up and take back our power and to restore ourselves to wholeness (holiness) and to gather our fragmented selves back into the sacred. Scales makes a distinction between eternity and immortality pointing out that the

---

[153] Sarton, *A Grain of Mustard Seed: New Poems*, p. 38.
[154] Caputi, "Anne Scales 'Imagines Us': From the Eco-pornographic Story to the Medusa Counternarrative", *University of Denver Law Review*.

male ego must make a mark, a scar on the female earth that somehow signifies his conquering of life, Nature and woman, rendering him immortal, defending against his fear of death. But eternity is the understanding of the cycle of life and that we are always a part of the eternal here and now in what Scales calls "mere specks in the plasma of the universe."

There are many feminist writers who have dissected the Medusa myth and have retold her story to empower women—and girls. Again, it would take volumes to cover this subject and the purpose of this article is to give an overview of some of this writer's views on this myth that has profoundly shaped womens' psyches for centuries.

As we move down the hallway of Medusa's mirrors hanging on the walls in human imagination, we come to an unusual reflection that is relatively unknown and rarely seen. In the beginning of this article, I mentioned that I felt the challenge in dealing with the cross-cultural woman-hating myths like the Medusa myth is finding what is at the core of such disturbing storytelling, most of which has been done by men—the victors in the battle of the change from women-centered cultures to patriarchy.

I have often wondered about the origins of myths from cultures around the world that seem to bear similar resemblances even though contact amongst people living far apart most likely did not occur. In sitting with this question, I have embarked on a journey for some time now looking for answers that might shed some light on this inquiry. In doing so, I have come across the work of a number of writers, scholars, mythologists and scientists (outside the box so to speak) who have opened my eyes about the cosmos and her stories and who have pointed me in an exciting direction where it feels like I am putting pieces of a puzzle together. That puzzle has to do with the origins of myth, which I believe are not made up stories. It seems that there is a high likelihood that certain myths that have come down to us through time are based on experiences our ancestors had when planetary configurations in our solar system were different than what we know and on observations of celestial skies that are not visible today.

Authors of *Hamlet's Mill: An Essay on Myth and the Frame of Time* Giorgio de Santillana and Hertha von Dechend posit that all myths are based on archeoastrology or astroarcheology, the study of the astronomical knowledge of prehistoric cultures:

> De Santillana and von Dechend interpret widely scattered myths with the assumption, which many now feel is essentially correct, that cosmological mythic narratives unfold, like given stories, from events observed in night sky. The most ancient myths, though cloaked in culture-specific garb or expressed via different creative metaphors, describe an identical underlying celestial map: "The places referred to in myth are in the heavens and the actions are those of celestial bodies. Myth, in short, was a language for the perpetuation of a vast and complex body of astronomical knowledge."[155]

Given that Medusa is part of a complex myth, the question comes to my mind: What was reflected in the skies that a myth about a "monstrous" female image could be created in "mankind's" imagination? And this myth was not just found in Classical Greece, as I have mentioned before. It is my contention that the global misogynist eruption occurred as a result of a catastrophic planetary shift that later became the basis of the story, as well as that of the emergence of patriarchy.[156] Mythologist David Talbott, author of *The Saturn Myth*, is in agreement with de Santillana and von Deschend. His work is inspired by the late Immanuel Velikovsky, author of *Worlds in Collision,* and many other works, who questioned the acceptance of mainstream science's notion that our solar system has always been the stable configuration we know

---

[155] Jenkins, "Commentary on Hamlet's Mill."
[156] A topic I am addressing in a forthcoming book.

today—i.e., that our planets were all born at the same time. They were not. He believed that our solar configuration has gone through changes that are ignored by mainstream science. Talbott says, "Velikovsky was the first to propose that the positions, motions, and relationships of planets have been fundamentally altered in geologically recent times."[157] Furthermore, Velikovsky believed that Venus was a comet that entered our solar system as an ejection from Jupiter (birth from Zeus' forehead since Jupiter was the Roman name for Zeus?) and created catastrophic events recorded in myth—i.e., floods, deluges, fire raining from the sky, etc. Since the time he wrote the book in 1950, which became a bestseller, he was shunned by the mainstream. However, since then space age exploration has discovered that many of his assertions are true. For instance, mainstream science has claimed that Venus is our sister planet with a cool surface. Velikovsky predicted that Venus was a new addition to our solar system and has a hot surface and a comet tail, indicating she is not our sister. Much to the surprise of current scientists, he was proven right by fairly recent Russian and NASA space missions to Venus.

Talbott's work and research on planet instability are extensive. It is his thesis that there was a certain age of myth-making around the world that reflected the planets as gods because he says what humans witnessed in the skies was both beautiful and terrifying. It is this reflection that I will focus on here. Talbott has teamed up with physicist and Electric Universe proponent Wallace Thornhill in creating a new approach to understanding how the universe works and how myths are seen in the context of the Electric Universe. Catastrophic disturbances that have occurred on Earth are reflected both in rock art from around the world as well as in myths. The painstakingly chiseled rock art reveals many forms and shapes that are unmistakable symbols of plasma discharges—massive high energy electrical arcing between planets seen in the sky by ancient humans that can be reproduced in the laboratory. Some of these

---

[157] Talbott, interview in Aeon Journal.

forms appear as thunderbolts, dragons, snakes and feathery serpents, ubiquitous around the globe. The reflection in this mirror I am discussing is the form Medusa has taken in "mankind's" imagination born out of catastrophe when Venus, known as the Mother Goddess in many cultures, changed her position in the sky and became the "terrible goddess." I feel this is the origin story of the hatred of women we also witness around the world. Catastrophe ensued on Earth when the planets—particularly Saturn, Venus and Mars, the celestial "gods"—experienced planetary instability, giving birth to the myths of wars amongst the anthropomorphized planet/gods. Prior to the catastrophe, the so-called Golden Age reigned and the planetary configurations in the sky were very different than what we now observe. Talbott explains,

> There was an "age of the gods" when the planets *were* the gods, and the entire story content of global mythology traces to this unique period... What global mythology gives us is a profile of the way humankind related to intense experiences of beauty and terror. [158]

This "age of the gods" Talbott names is what I would call the age of patriarchal gods—Classical Greek, Roman, Hindu and others. The important issue is that the myths are about anthro-pomorphized planets and the "wars" amongst them were visible interplanetary electrical encounters. Seen by the naked eyes of the ancients, Talbott writes that Venus was known as the hair star, the feathered or winged star, great flame and fiery serpent or dragon, which is a description of a comet with plasma discharge, validated by relatively recent space exploration:

> The "induced magnetotail" that points away from Venus in the direction of the earth is a teardrop-shaped plasma structure filled with "a lot of little stringy things" that was first detected by NASA's Pioneer Venus Orbiter in the late

---
[158] Talbott, interview in Aeon Journal.

1970's.[159]

It is not difficult to understand how the plasma ropes and "stringy things" could be seen as her snake hair. When planetary changes occurred, she was seen as the angry goddess attacking the world and as the "Doomsday Comet" and was considered the Mother of all Comets. Hence, the Medusa Archimage was born in the minds of the male scribes who have given us their mythical renditions of the ancient skies that are still taught in school today without the benefit of this understanding of witnessed celestial events. Myths of the warrior kings and dragon slayers also accompanied the story of the Medusa Archimage and there are countless cultural stories of male heroes slaying dragons and serpents across the globe, saving humanity from the angry, "demonic" goddess based on the anthropomorphized battles in the skies. The players in these myths were not people, though we treat some of them as if they were and study them as if we should make room for them to exist as such. Granted many metaphors and allegorical meanings of these myths do exist of course as numerous mythologists across the ages have offered their interpretations. However, cross- cultural rape mythology defies explanation in these terms though it has been accepted as normal behavior of male "gods." Though I do not accept rape mythology as anything worth teaching, I feel it is essential to understanding its origins.

Understanding the reflection in this mirror of Medusa requires a long and deep gaze, as I believe much of what has been taught about mythology in schools and universities is not accurate. I have only scratched the surface of this exploration. An in-depth comprehension of Electric Universe theory, plasma physics and the electrically connected universe requires a strong commitment and a willingness to let go of collective beliefs that are based on suppositions, assumptions and projections. [160] I am currently

---

[159] Van der Sluijs, "Venus' Tail of the Unexpected" at thunderbolts.info
[160] I do not subscribe to the mainstream theory of the Big Bang which is based on a gravity-driven universe and is considered by EU proponents to be a

involved in such an inquiry and invite the reader to find out more from my forthcoming book.

While Medusa does indeed hold many secrets, the one that has caught my attention now is how the mythology based on archeoastronomy in ancient cultures has affected who women are, how women are seen, and how women see themselves today. It is time to reclaim the essence of Medusa's sovereignty in her entirety, once again re-storying the Queen Serpent Goddess of Female Wisdom.

---

creation story adopted by mainstream science as fact. See Wallace Thornhill's youtube, "The Long Path to Understanding Gravity" and *The Big Bang Never Happened* by Eric Lerner.

REFERENCES:

Abraham, Karl, "Manifestations of the Female Castration Complex," in *Selected Papers of Karl Abraham*, Karl Abraham, Hogarth Press and the Institute of Psychoanalysis, London, 1942, p. 340.

Caputi, Jane, "Anne Scales 'Imagines Us': From the Eco-pornographic Story to the Medusa Counternarrative," *Denver University Law Review*, Vol 91, Issue 1, 2014.

Dexter, Miriam Robbins, "The Ferocious and the Erotic 'Beautiful' Medusa and the Neolithic Bird and Snake," *Journal of Feminist Studies in Religion*, Volume 26, Number 1, Spring 2010, p. 25.

Garcia, Brittany, "Medusa," http://www.ancient.eu/Medusa/ *Ancient History Encyclopedia*, 2013.

George, Demetra, *Mysteries of the Dark Moon* (HarperSanFrancisco, 1992), p. 155.

Jenkins, John Major, "Commentary on Hamlet's Mill."

Sarton, May, *A Grain of Mustard Seed: New Poems* (New York: Norton, 1971), p. 38.

Talbott, David, "Saturn Thesis," interview, *Aeon Journal, 1994*, aeonjoural.com

Van der Sluijs, Rens. "Venus' Tail of the Unexpected," thunderbolts.info, Feb 2008.

Walker, Barbara, *Women's Encyclopedia of Myths and Secrets* (Harper and Row, San Francisco, 1983), p. 721.

Pythic Portals
Nuit Moore

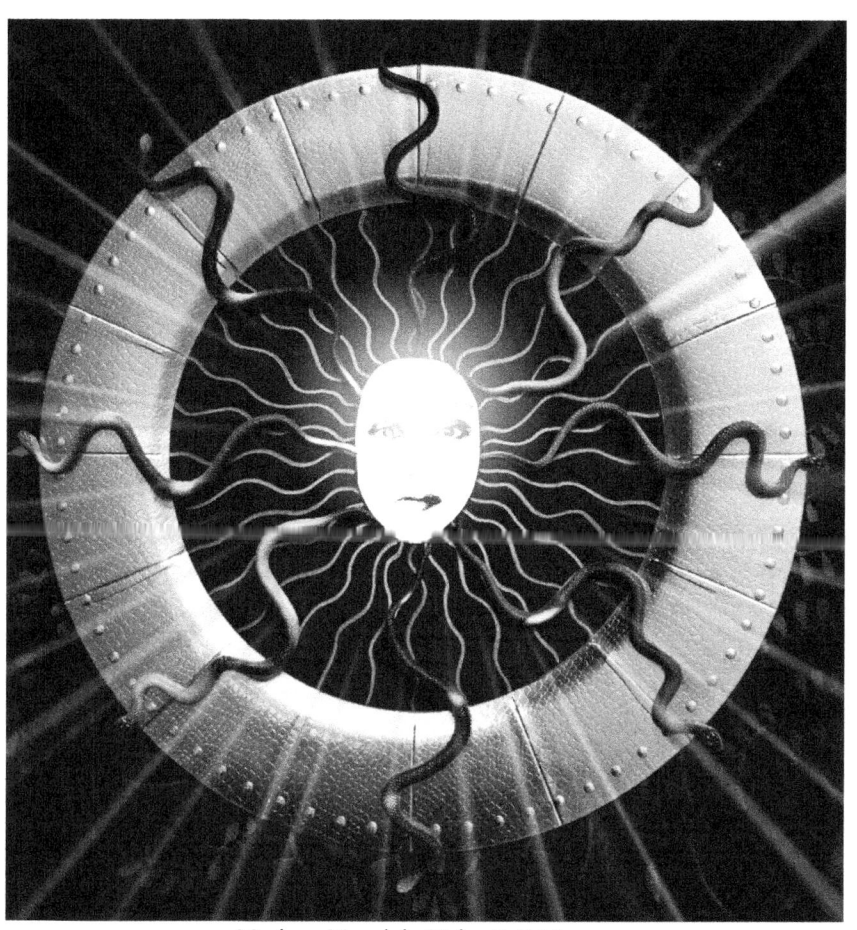

Medusa Mandala #1 by Nuit Moore

Medusa Mandala #2 – Nuit Moore

Medusa Mandala #3 – Nuit Moore

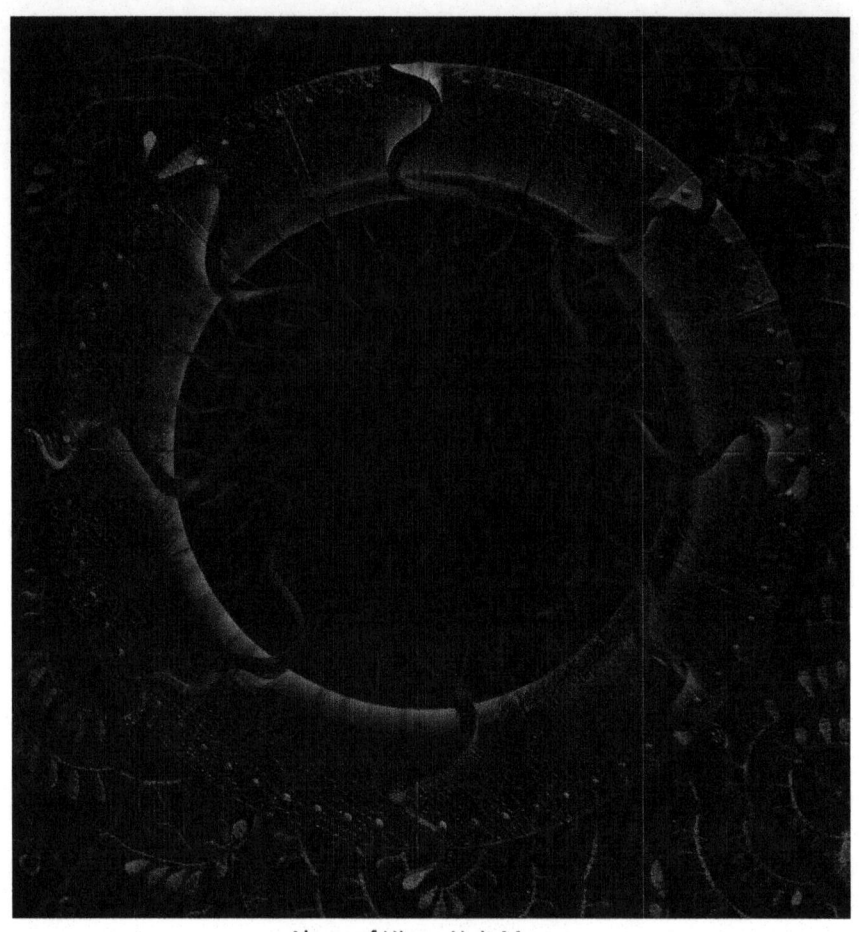

Abyss of Hiss – Nuit Moore

The Serpent Priestess knows intimately
the cycles of birth, life, death, rebirth...
transformation, regeneration, and renewal,
survival, the hiss within the abyss which stirs into being,
the hidden, the cave, the veil, the eclipse,
the depths of Earth and the bridges of stars,
the energy of ley lines of Gaia and body,
vibrational power and of Shakti rising,
the psyche sight of the third eye,
magick mirrors of shadow sky,
the prophetic utterance of scarlet oracle,
of sexuality, sensuality, fecundity, potency,
blood of womb, undulating howls of Medusa,
yonic kundalinic twinings, cobra cosmic spin,
leading deep into the initiation of deep within.

-Nuit Moore

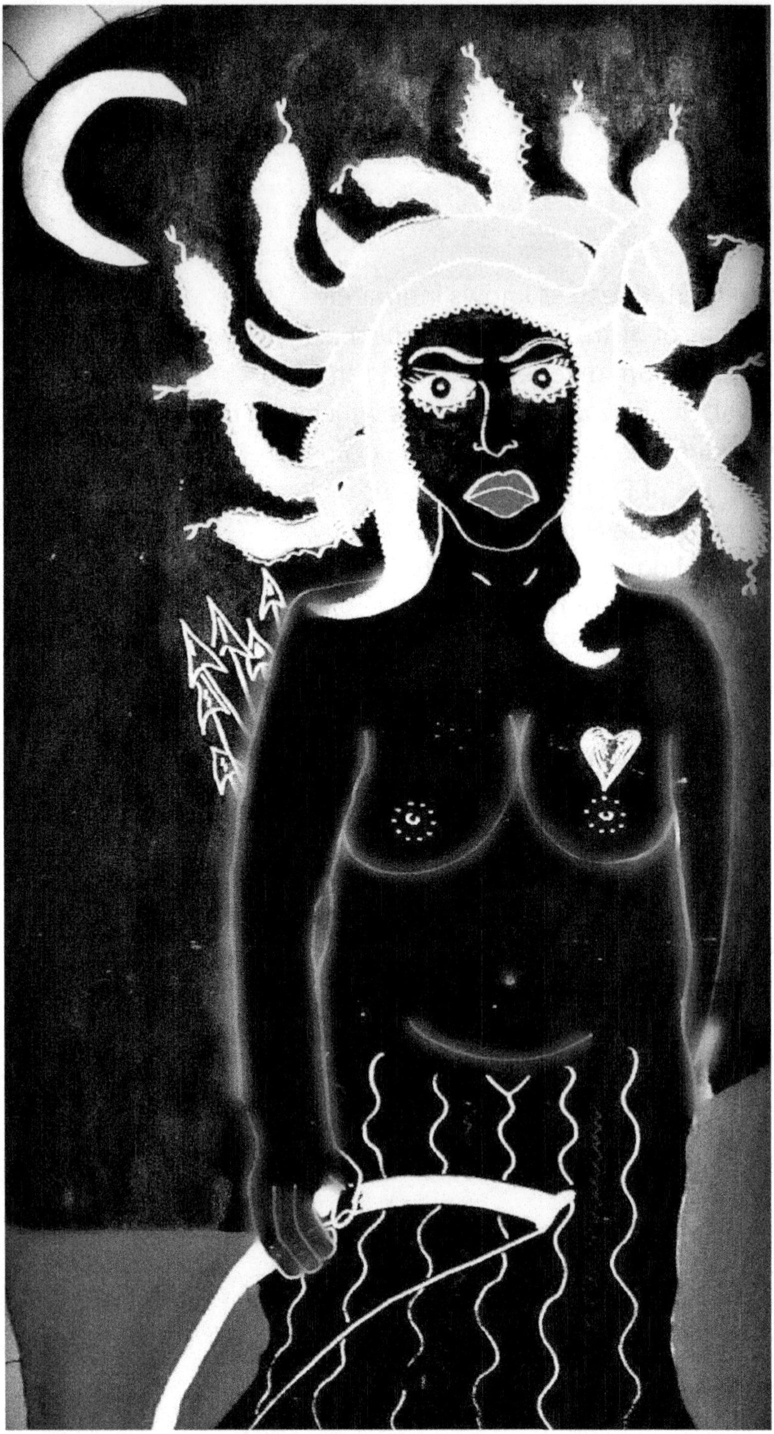

I painted this Medusa in 1997, with magickal intent behind Her. I had ended a 2-year relationship with someone after they physically assaulted me (by trying to strangle me, closing off my voice, at the neck, my hair streaming), and called me all of those words that weak men will call a strong woman. I wanted Medusa to have my back after he was taken to jail, after he was out of the house. So, one night on the next Dark Moon I painted Medusa with all of the rage and fierceness I felt. I wanted whoever would cause me harm to stop in their tracks when they saw Her eyes (which contained my eyes), to freeze and not be able to take another step into my home. And so, for many years, I kept this Medusa facing my front door. It is thought by some, including myself, that the serpent-tressed Gorgons found on the outside of some ancient temples indicated that this was a holy space of the mysteries of women and of the Goddess, and the Medusa served as Temple Guardian of these mysteries, and as a warning to those who would trespass. I actually did not even think of this when I painted Her to guard my own temple. It was instinctual, the call—and this is how She speaks, from the awakened kundalini... from the root of the yoni to the belly pit of survival and up through the opened third eye that sees. Medusa Herself is an ancient Libyan Goddess of the mysteries of Life and Death, regeneration, the menstrual mysteries, the shamanic powers of serpents and snakes.

Fierce and deeply powerful, the Goddess MEDUSA.

Pegasus as a Symbol of Transcendence
Arna Baartz

Ancient Wisdom for Modern Times
C. Loran Hills

ONCE UPON A TIME I lived in a tiny duplex on a street nicknamed "Baltic Avenue." My mattress rested on a floor that sloped toward the bathroom. Every morning, I stumbled downhill toward the toilet. My bedroom was also a magical place. Crystals hung in the Eastern window, illuminating the room with rainbows as the sun rose. Posters of Pegasus decorated the walls.

Enchanted by the image of a magical white horse with wings, I collected pictures and statues of Pegasus for years. I never considered the roots of Pegasus' story until recently. I'm more curious now about his origins than I was those many years ago. My search for knowledge provided surprising and relevant information that I wish I had known sooner.

Pegasus is a symbol of spiritual elevation, transformation, and transcendence. I always knew that Pegasus was born out of Medusa's blood but I didn't know the entire story. I followed that trail of blood toward a richer, deeper understanding of female power. When I read Barbara Walker's *Women's Encyclopedia of Myths and Secrets*, I discovered a complex and more meaningful narrative. Long ago, Medusa was the serpent-goddess of the Libyan Amazon. She represented female wisdom as the destroyer aspect of the Triple Goddess, Virgin-Mother-Crone. She was similar to Kali Ma, the Hindu Triple Goddess of creation, preservation and destruction.

A Gorgon was a monstrous female creature within the complicated pantheon of Greek gods and goddesses. Her face would turn anyone who laid eyes upon it to stone. Gorgons were hideous beings with impenetrable scales, hair of living snakes, hands made of brass and sharp fangs. They guarded the entrance to the underworld. A stone head or picture of a Gorgon was often placed or drawn on temples to avert the dark forces of evil. Medusa was one such Gorgon.

Medusa embodied the principle of *medha,* the Indo-European root word for female wisdom. Pegasus was named for the Pegae, water priestesses who tended the sacred spring of Pirene in Corinth, Greece. Pegasus represented divine inspiration. His crescent moon-shaped hoof stamped the ground and dug the Hippocrene (Horse-Well), a spring of poetic inspiration on Mount Helicon, the home of the Muses.

In a late version of the Medusa myth, related by the Roman poet Ovid (Metamorphoses 4.770), Medusa is a ravishingly beautiful maiden, "the jealous aspiration of many suitors." Poseidon rapes Medusa in Athena's temple. The enraged Athena transforms Medusa's beautiful hair into serpents and makes her face so terrible to behold that the mere sight of it turns onlookers to stone.

King Polydectes, the ruler of Seriphos, enters the story. He wants to marry Danaë, the only child of the king of Argos; however, her son, Perseus, doesn't approve. In an effort to get rid of Perseus, the king sends him to fetch Medusa's head, expecting him to die. Athena assists Perseus by giving him a mirrored shield. He views Medusa's reflection in the shield and cuts off her head. Immediately, Pegasus springs from Medusa's blood.

This latter version of the story is disturbing in that Medusa is blamed and punished by Athena even though she is Poseidon's victim. In another twist, Athena co-opts Medusa's power by placing Medusa's face upon her shield. Yet, after many millennia, Medusa remains a compelling symbol of wild female power. Paradoxically, she is a dangerous, unruly woman who invokes fear and she is also a potent image of inner strength for women.

Wild women are condemned as corrupt, depraved, immoral, sinful, wanton, and wicked. Women who live in a state of nature, not tamed or domesticated, are unruly, ungovernable, visionary, savage, and ferocious. These derogatory labels teach us to fear each other, our power, and to deny our inner wisdom. Strong-willed women are demonized in the patriarchal system and socialized to behave.

American historian Laurel Thatcher Ulrich pointed out that, "Well behaved women seldom make history." She lamented the fact that women who made positive impacts on society have been consistently overlooked in general education. We've been well-trained to behave, to stay in our place.

I have my own well-behaved past. In my family of origin, I was taught to be passive, compliant, and pleasing. I barely knew my own truth, and if I did, I was afraid to speak it. Feelings were never expressed. I wasn't provided any female models of wisdom or power.

When I was in graduate school, I took a life-altering class, *Women's Issues*. It was the equivalent of a 1970's consciousness-raising group. I learned about the oppression of women and the suppression of female power throughout the ages. For centuries, women have been schooled to disconnect from their ancient ways of knowing about their bodies, their intuition and the natural world with all its magic and mystery. Stories about wild women certainly weren't taught in my schools or church. These institutions continue to sustain patriarchal propaganda about the dominance of men and the subservience of women. Aversion and fear of our own menstrual blood, aging, and death are considered normal.

When it sank in how much women's history was omitted or distorted from my education, I was completely outraged. One day I went home and beat a towel around the house, screaming until I accidentally broke a lightbulb. Then, in a mad frenzy, I cleaned the entire house with all that energy.

During this same time, I studied martial arts and used karate to channel my rage. I felt the need to learn how to defend myself. Filled with self-righteous indignation, I sized up men as opponents and taunted them until a man set his own limits and put his boot about an inch away from my face. I learned then to tone it down a little but the anger still roiled within me.

Patriarchal mythology distorts the female forces of life and nature and sets out to destroy those forces in myriad ways. Whether or not dismantling the power of the goddess and the planet was deliberate is a topic for another essay. Either way, we've been socialized to perpetuate destructive forms of power, control, and intimidation.

As women, we must nurture one another, build each other up, and educate ourselves. Ancient and modern patriarchal stories have encouraged us to feel antagonistic toward and alienated from ourselves and other women. As women, we contain deep reservoirs of intuition and life-giving power. It's important that we shift our consciousness toward support, empathy, and understanding.

I've worked for more than three decades to transform my rage into spiritual growth. Repeatedly, I'm called to face my darkest emotions. I continue to read voraciously in order to educate myself about the ways in which patriarchal thinking has influenced my life. My experience and wisdom grows as I age. My inner power evolves as a result of my journey through life.

Clarissa Pinkola Estes wrote, "A good deal of literature on the subject of women's power states that men are afraid of women's power. I always want to exclaim, 'Mother of God! So many women themselves are afraid of women's power.'" Divine female forces are vast and formidable. Not only have we been conditioned to fear our own power, sometimes we fear other women and tear them down. Women's mythology provides inspiration for a more meaningful journey into wholeness and understanding.

Long ago, it was believed that women became wise when they no longer shed the lunar "wise blood" but kept it within. Our power as women was tied to the "blood mysteries." We bleed without dying and bear children. These mysteries have been long misunderstood and vilified. Each stage of our development, from maiden to mother then crone, has its own significance. The fear of aging is rampant in Western society. As a post-menopausal woman, I can't help but notice how aging is viewed as repugnant. Aging is seen as pathology and treated like a disease. Women are terrified of turning into "hags" when, in fact, female power grows with age.

Hag originally meant "holy woman," queen of the dead, incarnate on earth. The famous Byzantine structure in Istanbul, Hagia Sophia, translates as holy wisdom. Historically, a hag has no male form or counterpart. She is a diviner, a soothsayer, a woman of prophetic and oracular powers.

The hedge was once considered the boundary between the "civilized" world and the wild keepers of primal mysteries. The Hag is She Who Straddles the Hedge. Today, the word hag is defined as an ugly old woman, especially a vicious or malicious one. Sadly, now the hag brings up feelings of revulsion instead of reverence.

Medusa was fearsome. She represented Death and to see her face was to die; turning to stone symbolized dying and becoming a funerary statue. Pegasus, born from her magical blood, led me to her. Medusa is a Holy Hag, not a monster. She is a Wise Woman and a Guardian of the Divine Dark. I feel a strong affinity with Medusa and compassion for her story. Her snakes are not evil. They are a symbol of transformation. She doesn't fear her divine power. She is a timeless guardian of magic and healing. Medusa is a protector of women's wisdom, a protector we need now more than ever. I long for her potent, transformative energy to enter our world.

I'm integrating Medusa as a wild and powerful part of myself. If we, as ferocious women, learn to embrace our wild nature and capacity for the full range of emotions—if we don't turn away— we can dismantle patriarchal conditioning. Inner female power grows from the Divine Dark, the Underworld, where our earthy parts of self remain until we bring them to the light of day.

Vicki Noble, creator of the *Motherpeace Tarot Deck*, states that to "break free of the chains that bind us to old habit patterns and stuck ways of thinking requires an Amazon consciousness, a Medusa-like focus on victory." Behaviors and attitudes of the past are no longer valid for us. We need to courageously speak up for ourselves and each other.

Medusa encourages us to transform ourselves, to grow spiritually, and offers Pegasus as a symbol of transcendence. Medusa invites us to cope with our fear, terror, and rage, to confront our resistance to aging, and to challenge the negative thinking about our wild female nature. The question is, will we accept her invitation?

As we move into a new era sociologically and politically, we could be called to engage in civil disobedience. Kali Akuno, the Director of Human Rights Education at the U.S. Human Rights Network, states, "If we are serious and steadfast, we can create a clear and comprehensive message around being ungovernable." Challenged to reframe our culture, we will need Medusa-like ferocity to fight for human rights, to turn outmoded ways of thinking into stone.

Perhaps Medusa doesn't speak to you as clearly as she speaks to me. It's possible that you might need to do your own research on powerful women, goddesses and priestesses. I encourage you to find your own inner guide and symbol of female power. Call upon her when you feel the need for strength and assistance. She will answer you.

French feminist writer, Hélène Cixous wrote, "You only have to look at the Medusa straight on to see her. And she's not deadly. She's beautiful and she's laughing."[161] Medusa, crowned with the snakes of transformation, wise from experience, is laughing in ecstasy, inspiring us to live a courageous, powerful existence.

---

[161] Cixous, Hélène. "The Laugh of the Medusa," translated by Paula and Keith Cohen. 1976.

Medusa on Big Tree
Glenys Livingstone Ph.D.

Artist unknown
MoonCourt, Blue Mountains

Close-up by Glenys Livingstone Ph.D. / Artist unknown.
MoonCourt, Blue Mountains

How You Can Reattach Medusa's Head
Marguerite Rigoglioso, Ph.D.

THIS ARTICLE IS A CALL TO ACTION and to healing for those who have felt deeply disturbed by the beheading of Medusa and know that the ripples of that event still affect us today.

On March 22, 2012, Medusa's head was reattached in a ritual. From the esoteric perspective, this event was real and has had ripple effects throughout the time/space hologram.

You are invited to participate in and reinforce this critical re-membering through what follows. Your own actions will similarly have real effects that will contribute to the healing of the Feminine and the entire fabric of world reality. The invitation is open to people of all genders.

The setting for this event was my Divine Birth Mystery Teachings program, held that Thursday evening in El Cerrito, CA. For nearly a decade now, I had felt called to perform this sacred act in concert with other women, and my module on Athena seemed the right time. The ritual was created by Kathy Stanley and assisted by Elizabeth Fogge, with participation from all of the women in the program.

Kathy had designed a cloth effigy of Medusa, had ritually beheaded her in her own private ceremony, and had brought the pieces and laid them out before us on an altar. Then, she invited each of us to come up, take the needle and thread, and offer several stitches to reattach her head at the neck, as everyone chanted, drummed, and rattled. At the end, we collectively uttered ululations, also known as the *ololugué* in ancient Greek, or the Arabic *zagarit*—a trilling cry made with the tongue that was part of the worship of Athena. The deed was (un)done. At last.

The Significance of the Be/Re-Heading
Many of us have been absolutely horrified by the story of Medusa's head being cut off by the so-called hero Perseus, and then buried in the marketplace at Argos. We know there is something here that is terribly pernicious for women. In Medusa's beheading we are dealing with the tremendous disempowerment of one of our most potent ancestors, a living high holy ruler who was brought to shattering and humiliating defeat at the hands of the encroaching patriarchal establishment. The shockwaves of that story have continued to be felt for millennia. And the act has been perpetrated and re-perpetrated in numerous stories and films, re-enlivening what amounts to the beheading of all women, over and over again, through verbal and visual repetition. Beware of such tales and films on the energetic level.

But women have now literally taken the matter into their own hands. With the enactment of this reparatory ritual, we set in motion the re-memberment of this ancestor, and thus the reversal of her story. With that, we set into motion the reversal of the story of all women's disempowerment. Take that in for a moment…

How You Can Help with the Cosmic "Do Over" and Future Seeding
As Founding Director of Seven Sisters Mystery School, I put out the call for a global "Medusa Re-Memberment Activation." This means I have invited people all over the world to enact their own Medusa re-heading rituals so as to energetically reinforce and affirm this "do-over" of history. I envision this activity as a new kind of "Vagina Monologues" for the post-2012 rebirth era. I inspire you to create pageants, performance art, and social action around such rituals.

I am also inviting you to engage in a periodic three-minute meditation that is very simple: Close your eyes and see Medusa before you. Visualize her kundalini track being fully restored from her yoni all the way up and out to the tips of her snakey hair, strengthened like a nerve being restored. The effect is magnified if you do it in a group.

In reinforcing this vision, you participate not only in re-membering Medusa, but also in restoring the kundalini circuit among the chakras for yourself and ALL women. And that means you join in the great worldwide project to help women reintegrate mind and body, sexuality and spirituality, heaven and earth.

It is now time to get busy. Don't sit idly by, merely lamenting the abuses of patriarchy. Close your eyes and create the change through the incredible power of your visioning mind. Your efforts WILL positively influence our future.

Italy's Mass Medusa Re-memberments
My book, *The Cult of Divine Birth in Ancient Greece* was issued in Italy in 2013 as *Partenogenesi: Il Culto della Nascita Divine nell'Antica Greca* (Psiche 2, Turin), and in February 2013 I went to Italy to do talks and workshops to launch it.

Meanwhile, my brilliant book translator and event co-producer, Valeria Trisoglio, keyed into the blog post I did in 2012 discussing the ritual my students did to reattach the head of Medusa. She heeded my invitation for people all over the world to enact their own Medusa re-heading rituals so as to energetically reinforce and affirm this "do-over" of history and organized 15 cities to conduct these rituals all over Italy in 2013!

The idea began in Rome, with women and men enthusiastically planning and participating, and has spread from the Alps to Sicily in cities such as Arezzo, Biella, Bologna, Genova, Lucca/Pisa, Mantova, Messina, Milano, Napoli, Palermo, Parma, Pomezia, Torino, and Udine. Events began with a lecture and PowerPoint packet developed from my writings on Medusa in *The Cult of Divine Birth in Ancient Greece*, followed by sacred rituals with effigies of decapitated Medusas in various materials (clay, cardboard, fabric, etc.), which they solemnly re-headed. Valeria also provided a chant, which some groups sang: "*Morte e vita, veleno e cura Lei trasforma e fa paura. Regina e donna, Dea Serpente Medusa è integra e potente.* Death and life, poison and cure She transforms and instills fear Queen and woman, Serpent Goddess Medusa is whole and powerful."

The experience was powerful and moving in every city. The round of rituals concluded on February 14, 2013, in Milan, which connected it with the global 1 Billion Rising movement spearheaded by Eve Ensler to end violence against women. I was in Milan presiding over that re-memberment ritual! Many thanks to Valeria and all of the Italian women and men who joined this powerful movement. Please encourage your friends around the world to create their own Medusa re-memberment rituals.

Medusa's Vindication (it will be the mirror)
Kerryn Coombs-Valeontis

from the imprisonment of her violation
vipers crowning the exile hiss
a fury that can never
be captured

devouring her dementing well beyond
the sanity of rage, banished
of innocence, her revenge poised
to strike; hunted becomes the hunter

clever one's journey
seeking renown, eager to vanquish
the scorned woman that becomes the gorgon
withering the bravest

it will be the mirror, holding truth
to their lie; the sword its servant
releasing its prey from the sins
of the fathers

ransomed to their shame, she hears
the wing-beats of the white
horse, sprung from her spilt
vindication draining away...

bearing her far beyond vengeance
leaving those who do not mourn
burning to possess the purity
of the Pegasus ascending

Medusa's Mask (shield) of Righteous Rage
Kerryn Coombs-Valeontis

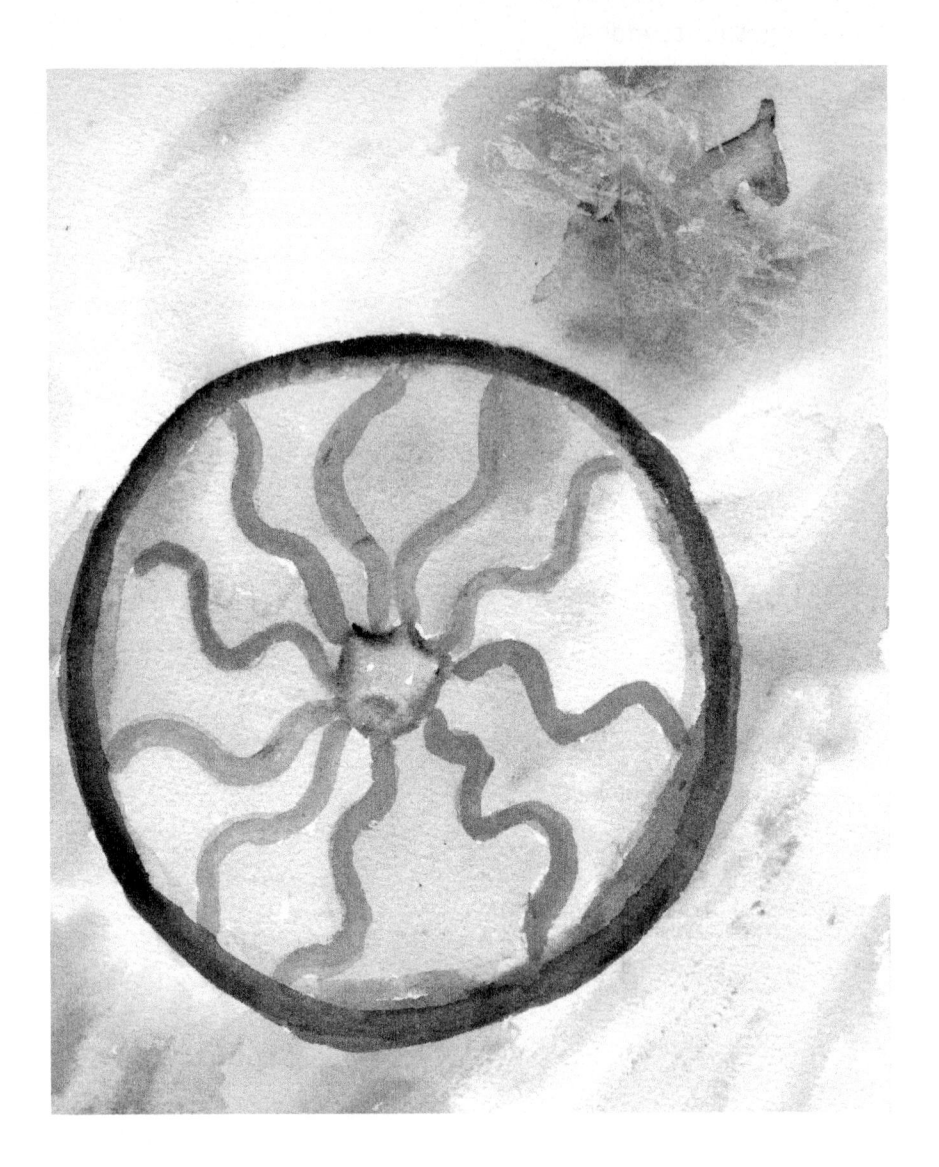

Medusa's Mask of Righteous Rage

Kerryn Coombs-Valeontis

i wear medusa's mask
the righteous rage of it—(not righteous indignation
or anger—it is more furious than that)
because you can't go around
being that angry—it needs a shield or it would
wither those who bothered with it
or tripped over it
it does burn those who look in—
those who love me most, do that
and i burn again each time, with
them—yet it is my ally
defending me in the loneliness
of being right—a victim's place
of vindication
her only option when such violation
blows the circuit breaker of truth
but i sometimes dream of winged
horses and think I can feel feathers
brush my face...

Winged Beast
Caroline Alkonost

Medusa: Wisdom of the Crone Moon

Theresa Curtis, Ph.D.

ALL MYTH IS AN UNFOLDING of both being and becoming. Hence, Medusa equally *was*—as Herself, precisely—and *is*—brewing Her story as circumstances warrant. I do Her a disservice when I dissect and mold Her into a specimen of interpretation. In face, Medusa is fierce, turning to stone those whose interest is superficial. As Goddess, She can unravel Her deeper medicine beyond time and space for those who ask—and it is toward this Medusa I intend to visit. How She chooses to venture forth today is Her business. But how we collaborate, intuit, circumambulate Her is all our affair, and I invite each of us to join this adventure.

We could honor Medusa as the three phases of Moon, and therefore the traditional three phases of Women: Maiden, Mother, and Crone. Various tales have told of Medusa's Maiden voyage toward lost innocence through rape (forced entry), and then Her radical Mothering moment when She births from Her bloody neck. Her tale is long and rich, and constantly unfurling deeper—it can never truly be known. Yet Medusa chooses which wisdom She imparts to each explorer, and She has visited specifically as a snake-headed, wisdom-infested Crone. For me, She reeks of the endless mystery of the secrets beyond the dark moon. Her mystical powers deliver terror to those who think they can reach Her through direct observation. Freud observed Medusa at length, interpreting Her as *Vagina dentata,* exhibiting panic and horror (stoning) in the face of Her power. In fact, he was never able to complete his treatise on Her.

Athena's (logic, order) rage ignites Medusa's power, wherein Medusa seems to pulsate with the unobservable might of sagacity —the Dark Crone Moon—and its deep endlessness of insight (in-sight) and possibility. She does not take lightly that wisdom is being stolen through measurable, evident reasoning. Rather, if we forego our gaze in order to perceive Her through reflection, then She may forego her head and birth Pegasus and Chrysaor. Medusa must be seen reflectively; only then is the fierce vision alive with the transformative energy of snake. She entices me in. If you are still reading this, then She is enticing you too.

Power of the Archetypal Medusa
Gather up, sisters. We must reflect upon Medusa without statuing to stone. It's time to find our voices—all of us, as women. Medusa is open for business: to accept Her voyagers and be discovered. Medusa offers a pulsating transformation—a deeper knowledge. Shall we undertake this mission? Yes, this is an adventure wrought with hedonism, angst, and enlightenment; it is not for the faint of heart. We shall reflect upon that which brings up our great fears; we will each touch our own distress—feel it; swim in it. We need a gritty honesty and willingness to open our minds to a deeper discovery. And when we are complete, we can birth our own Pegasus and Chrysaor. Only then will Medusa's story evolve.

How shall we ready for such a journey?

I have relied on intuition, ritual, and meditation to sense the brew of Medusa—and to trust Her. She is not easy to trust. And yet, She is predictable: if I am merely here to ogle, I will get stoned and nowhere. But when I honor and reflect upon Her, She is ripe with the guidance of Crone. Medusa has responded to effort and willingness. Yet She also instigates, in which I am the effect to Her cause. She is not only approaching me; She is enticing me to enter Her. This can feel like being swallowed, and then shat-out after being transformed through digestion. It is *as if* I am entering Medusa as Vagina Dentata, hungry and toothed. Facing Medusa requires courage.

I have wielded to an inclination to transform, to realize more of who I am, to alchemize. But alchemy is a patriarchal representation of the active Medusa; it is a masculine attempt to convert rigid iron to a more malleable and valuable gold. It relegates magic to science. Animus alchemy can measure, clarify, and change the visible surface—but Medusa's Crone wisdom does not live there; thus, alchemy and science will never illuminate the active Medusa. She is wrought only through reflection and contemplation.

It was by reflection, and refusing to merely gaze, that my great wombing within Medusa began. I have given of myself to Her that She may deliver to me my own Cronehood—where Her snakes may weave me a more fertile field to sidewind through. And so, I prepare for this Medusation—where the surface persona can be infused with a more essential knowing.

"*BE Medusa.*" Let her live in your curls for a while and see what wisdom you can bring up and add to the potion. Meditate on her. Sharpen your intuition through introversion, meditation, imagination. Leave Her some space to crawl in through your cracks. What you learn is your lesson—this is my personal learning:

Grounding my Self before stepping into the Myth

> *Without witnesses… people become trapped in silences* (Shulman-Lorenz, n.d., para 9).

I feel an obligation to sufficiently prepare and ground myself (I am, after all, an experiment) prior to mindfully responding to the initial rumblings of Medusa calling me inward; I link with my familiars before I connect with the unknown. Entering this transformational phase can be hazardous, and a way to process the sometimes overwhelming world of unconsciousness is essential. Marie-Louise von Franz notes the hazards one might encounter:

> When the conscious and unconscious personalities approach each other, then there are two possibilities: either the unconscious swallows consciousness, when there is a psychosis, or the conscious destroys the unconscious with its theories, which means a conscious inflation...and then people get out of it by saying the unconscious is 'nothing but...' (1980, p. 164)

Setting the Intention

Willingness to enter Medusa's Crone portal initiated an ego-confrontation between my individual self, and my Higher Self. Fear fought that call again and again, yet a commitment and trust in Medusa gave Her the upper hand, and She could then call my ego beyond itself. This also sets the stage for my little life to blow apart—to decrease my ego and make room for infinite creative divinity. Empty my cup, so to speak. The length of this fight is the breadth and width of my offering to Medusa. I struggled mightily and even unknowingly against this unpredictable freefall. I have hence learned that to *enter*, all I need do is stop, and turn toward Her. She will provide the journey—I need merely be present. What was I running from anyway? A story? Stop running and diverting! Be still and enter courageously into the vast empty. Turn toward what I avoid "facing," or feeling, and... reflect.

Induction

I sense Medusa's fire stirring within; I pause and listen as She infuses this message to me: "Become Medusa."

I contemplate, envisage, and let Her energy settle within and without my skin. I shudder with the suddenness of the conversion, and then image myself laden with hair-snakes flailing and hissing. I undergo an immediate transformation—I am Medusa!

I experience power! I feel courage, meaning, and confidence replace my earlier uneasiness. There is no room for fear here.

I have tapped into a vast vein of Crone's gold. I can accept it, and stop pretending I am either vicious, afraid, or impotent when threatened. Medusa's wisdom is wild and ferociously guarded. And if Medusa is the personification of that which humanity fears, abhors, and vilifies, then I also accept that within myself. Crone. the wide open, but daring, dark and deep. She opens the secret of Her wild mouth, caged with savage fangs. Not a very inviting portal, but a portal nonetheless—of entry, and exit. I invite Medusa and She accepts; I have begun my reflection. I find that knowledge and experience coexist. In order to expand my wisdom, I must also expand beyond mere vision. I must step outside the box I live in. When I move beyond the initial adventure, I find myself in an upended life and I lose my sense of self. I become depressed and suspicious and am afraid I will not move past this rigid stultifying state.

Yet I have learned that my inner Medusa is worthy of trust. I need to believe She can restore me to balance before I sink into some deeper wisdom of Crone.

> *I now find myself pulled into a quicksand of anxiety and fear—like a small craft on an endless sea.*
>
> *I fall for miles into Medusa's gaping mouth. I unwittingly, from every point imaginable, push hard to manage this descent into unbounded confusion and fear. But the underworld Hades has my tail, dragging me down. I have no control. I feel completely powerless.*
>
> *I feel so alone… lost and crazy. Where? Where is this precious Goddess I had grown to trust? Ah, You betrayer! I am tangled deep in a dark pit and falling deeper. Angry! Resentful! And… sad sad sad. Is there no end to this descent? Nothing works, nothing works. I am disintegrating. I can do nothing. I know nothing. I'll never know Medusa, I'll never know wisdom. I am turned into a frozen and lazy stone.*

This sense of powerlessness is a force greater than ego, and I cannot heal this disease in my ego *with* my diseased ego—but try I do. This utter lack of individual domination leaves me as a jigsaw puzzle, the box is open and every piece is unlinked. I lose my self to incongruence. I have been inducted.

Awareness
Awareness eventually simmers a shaky but steady stew, brewed from my commitment to trust this soup will nurture me with a spicier truth. The extraneous ingredients of my ego have now begun to evaporate out, and something new is cooking. This means that I have begun shaking free from my ego identity to melt into the expansiveness of Self. In *awareness* "I am" in a truer sense and have a more genuine place within the circle of life; I am something physical connected to some way mythical. *Awareness* is a symbolic expression for the rising of the light at the depth of darkness… when, in the depth of human crisis, change is birthed.

Becoming more psychologically whole involved falling apart into fear and confusion—into "not knowing," and accepting Medusa as guide and you, dear reader, as witness. Without an "Other" we are merely a tree falling in the forest which is never heard.

Medusa is teaching me that She, you, life, or my personage as a psychological "One" is limited. The Goddess needs us, and we, Her. But alone Medusa is merely an Anima passage, passive with mighty potentiality. Yet as Goddess she is a throbbing seductress inviting us to consider reflection as wisdom. Instead of ogling Her with vision, rather we can envision. *Perhaps it is She who will initiate the great unfurling of wisdom necessary to transform stone into a "Golden" Age.*

This I learned this from the process of trying to honor Medusa:
I am learning that more than anything: it is necessary to turn toward, and not away from, whatever adventure that life has set

before me. Turn toward pain, turn toward rage, turn toward sorrow, reality, terror, and the great emptiness that threatens to chew me up from the inside out. It is, ironically, this agonizing turning toward and courageous entering into that brings the hope of relief. Only then can I land somewhere outside my former edge of reality. This is acceptance, awareness, and allowance on the psychic level; this is the message received from Medusa the Crone. All I need do is ask, to invite Crone wisdom to guide—and then act on the guidance.

I am trusting that as myself I am entering Her as woman and need never resist inflowing when She sings me forward. I can discern Medusa's song as a welcoming siren. Medusa Herself is secure, predictable, and wise… whether I enter or not She remains intact. She will continue to beckon me toward ever-deepening wisdom, and I, as an initiate, need not fearfully flee.

Conclusion

My journey involved an experience of mind mud, which had oozed from the crumbling morsels of uncontrollable binge-eating, an escape that I was utterly powerless to regulate. Seduced by sugar, my psyche was constricted and squeezed. All my energy flattened into gray, and I reduced my life mana to complete one mission: to numb-out suffering and seek comfort. I tried every trick to control myself, but the terrifying addiction was greater than my brilliant guiles. Yet all this I experienced as I was writing Medusa forward (however incompletely), trusting She could deliver me to my Crone wisdom.

And now She is singing me toward and I can "hear." I know I am wrapped in guidance and can stretch my limits a bit.

Now I am hiking with my grandson and climb an unstable stack of rock that I normally would not. I feel I am making my way up the bouldered face of Medusa. I lean into a certain space that imaginally signifies Her toothed and open mouth. Surprisingly, it is cool and comforting. I sink Her rhythms in, then continue to climb. Above there is a little flat spot, just wide enough for my bum to settle. Ah! Meditation time. Reflection.

To me, this is the parthenogenic creation of the great Crone. Entering Medusa is entering into wisdom.

The word *initiation* comes from the Latin *initium* which means "entrance" or "beginning," literally "a going in." After the experience of emptying-out, or "not knowing," I was finally opened to receive the gifts of transformation. Within Medusa was the magnetic egg that is constantly inviting some unsuspecting ego in, toward Her mystery. I am saying that turning toward, and into, is a response to the siren song of Medusa; it is the action surrounding Her.

Medusa provides one with Crone wisdom—and a transformative path of reflection to consider. This "wombing" process can beckon one into accessing a wise inner directive that is as transformative as a snake shaking out of her skin. For the individuating divine feminine it is also a heraic journey.

Now I am birthing, solidifying, stoning (through writing) this experience forward. This is my twirling spiral into and out of the archetype of Medusa. This is a journey of trust and guidance. Dream images, rituals, cave mouth, snake, connects me to the everlasting Medusa. Past Her lips and onward She holds a tremendous elixir of life. She is not to be entered into lightly.

REFERENCES:

Gole, Chetan. (2017). *Medusa.* Retrieved May 1, 2017, from http://www.scaryforkids.com/medusa/

Shulman-Lorenz, H. (n.d.) *Amnesia/countermemory.* Retrieved October 11, 2010, from
http://www.pacifica.edu/gems/whenhistorywakes/Lorenz.pdf

von Franz, Marie-Louise. (1980). *Alchemy: An introduction to the symbolism and the Psychology.* Boston: Shambhala Publications.

Medusa Resume
Marie Summerwood

RÉSUMÉ

Medusa

POSITION SOUGHT: Goddess of Fierceness and Protection

PROFESSIONAL EXPERIENCE:
- Many generations as a Gorgon Priestess, guardian of womyn's blood mysteries.
- Serpent Goddess of the Libyan Amazons, descended from Lamia, the Libyan Serpent Goddess of Creation.
- Crone/Destroyer aspect of Neith, Triple Goddess in Egypt.

BACKGROUND:
- My name Medusa comes from many linguistic roots meaning "female wisdom."
- Gorgon priestesses wear masks with fierce countenances and serpents for hair. This represents the protective power we wield.
- "Fierce" means wild and proud; Fierce as the mother bear, the protector Fierce as the old womyn, the crone, the giver of death.

STRENGTHS:
- Ability to come forward in fierceness, or deadly anger if necessary.
- Ability to bring into the world outrage instead of rage, untamed beauty instead of armor.
- Ability to, with one look, frighten men into stony terror.
- Proven ability to inspire womyn.
- Highly adept at holding your back as you stand in your power.

LANGUAGES:
- I speak Passion and Fierceness; I sing the sacred chants of womyn.

SALARY REQUIREMENTS:
- Your attention, paid to Me, to My hand on your back, and to My energy rising up in you. Chant to Me.

Medusa's Stunning Powers Reflected in Literature
Dr. Gillian M.E.(dusa) Alban

THE MONSTROUSLY DIVINE MEDUSA is emblematic of women's struggles to rise above oppressions with her serpentine power and invincible gaze. Seen as the dark aspect of female divinity, Miriam Robbins Dexter defines Medusa as the "ruling one" who represents the "Neolithic Goddess of birth, death and regeneration" (Dexter 25), while Susan Bowers describes Medusa as "an electrifying force representing the dynamic power of the female gaze" (Bowers 235). This writing discusses the stunningly defiant gaze of the monstrous Medusa beaming out through the characters of women writers, her irresistible power apotropaically, that is, turning her force back against her foes in becoming an inspirational power for women.

Despite the social advances made in Western societies, women largely remain the second sex under the castigation of patriarchal founding myths and mind frames. Yet Eve's initiative brings about human entrance into this world, and the feistily independent Lilith offers women a tremendous model in her refusal of Adam's demands. Female values slighted and their physical and sexual vulnerability abused, men have reported their own history, ignoring herstory. Despite the Genesis account of God being an androgyne, since he created men and women equally in his or her own image, at the same time declaring Eve to be the mother of all living, the fable of God creating Eve from Adam's rib is still largely accepted. Yet D. H. Lawrence through Anna Lensky in *The Rainbow* asserts woman's unique capacity to give birth, thus: "It is impudence to say that Woman was made out of Man's body, when every man is born of woman. What impudence men have, what arrogance!" (Lawrence 174). The founding myth of Adam and Eve actually shows ancient proof of womb envy, with men emulating women's ability to bear new life, which they still cannot achieve, despite any Frankenstein attempts.

Medusa was raped by Poseidon in the Temple of Athena, yet she arises above this devastation. The male-disposed Athena, denying Metis, her own maternal source, and defending the mother-slaughter of Clytemnestra, punishes the innocent rape victim Medusa. Yet even as Medusa's hair is turned into snakes, she assumes an enigmatic power as she is transformed into a staring snake woman. Medusa's punishment of snakes for hair is similar to the 'curse' placed on the fairy Melusine, who is 'gifted' or more accurately 'empowered' by her mother with having a snake's tail below her waist each Saturday (Alban, "Serpent Goddess" 32). The Medusa complex of "hissing snakes" (Louise Bogan, "Medusa") and an indomitable gaze that no one can face, actually affords Medusa a tremendous serpentine life force. The cowardly Perseus beheads Medusa as she is sleeping, with Athena guiding his shaking hand. Baring and Cashford suggest that striking off Medusa's head through the mirroring view of his shield reveals Perseus' fear of her as one that actually emerges from himself (Baring and Cashford 342). The consequences of her being "so rudely forced" (T. S. Eliot, *The Waste Land*) by the equine Poseidon emerge from her savaged neck in the shape of the winged Pegasus and Chrysaor the warrior. M[ed]usa or the Muse becomes mother to Pegasus, wellspring of the muses of art and poetry, her erotic and inspirational force particularly shown in proliferating Medusa figures.

Raped and murdered, Medusa's divine powers live on through her powerfully destructive gaze. This indomitable gaze enables women to reconstitute their psyche in tougher, resilient forms. Although men abrogate the power of their own gaze against women, objectifying them as mere bodies and placing women under male violence, men quail before the petrifying gaze and snaky hair of Medusa, attempting to diminish Medusa even as they assert their own gaze against her. Bowers states that men "make Medusa—and by extension, all women—the object of the male gaze as a protection against being objectified themselves by Medusa's female gaze" (Bowers 220). The male gaze often attempts to deny the creative psychic and intellectual force of women, regarding her instead as a horrific monstrosity.

The splendid paintings of Frida Kahlo show the defiant Medusa stare of this extraordinary artist returning her gaze back onto the viewer, reversing the male appropriation of the gaze. After the ghastly tramway accident that very nearly destroyed her, Kahlo with her mother's help set up a huge mirror over her bed enabling her to repeatedly paint her own face, each portrait recording a milestone in her agonizing life. Defiantly projecting her gaze out from her portraits, she immortalizes herself in multiple scenes, staring out at us powerfully beyond time. Kahlo describes herself as ugly, yet her extraordinary beauty and presence beam out through her magnificent artistic creations. This is shown in the Kahlo Medusa, magnificently presented here in Meg Dreyer's illustration (p. 176).

The petrifying Medusa gaze is exemplified in Toni Morrison's *Beloved*, as the helpless slave Sethe returns her gaze back onto her oppressors while trying to save her children's lives against impossible odds. Sethe undergoes incredible torture at 'Sweet Home' as first her baby's milk is stolen—how defensive she is of her child's right to her own mother's milk. Then, despite her advanced pregnancy, her back is whipped into an insensate pulp, becoming a veritable tree of scars. Who would imagine that this pregnant woman could rise up from such suffering to walk alone to freedom and reach her three children who need her? Dragging herself to where she can bear her latest child, she finally crosses the Ohio River where she technically becomes free, although this means nothing to the legalized forces of slavery that objectify human beings into the property of others. After a brief respite, the four riders of the apocalypse approach the new home of Sethe, where she outfaces the white man.

When Sethe recognizes Schoolteacher, she only has one thought in her mind, and that is to prevent, refuse, make it impossible for him to cart away her precious load of beloved children and turn them back into his slaves. If this inhuman man gets possession of them, he will abuse and persecute them as his property, scattering them across the land. Sethe makes the ultimate 'rough choice' of destroying her children, taking them out of this cruel world to a place where no slaver can follow them, beyond slavery, suffering, even life itself, beyond the further shedding of blood. Hearing the wings of the apocalypse telling her that the end of her world has come and extreme conditions apply, she determines that her precious family will not return to Schoolteacher's oppression. The word NO reverberating in her head, she exercises her power over her children to ensure that the lives she created are 'safe.' Sethe slashes the neck of her most precious daughter, Beloved, and lashes out at her sons, who fall 'dead' to the ground amongst their own and their sister's blood. She is still swinging her new baby helplessly against the wall to remove her from the misery of becoming the property of another, as all eyes turn on her in horror, and Stamp Paid snatches her baby out of her loving, desperate arms. Schoolteacher watches, the sheriff poises to execute justice, the slave hunter awaits his prey. Stepping beyond them all in this terrible act, which a mother should never do but which only a mother can do, she determines that she will not surrender her children to such suffering, regardless of the cost. With the beheaded child tucked in her arms, she reaches out to feed her new baby. Refusing to put down her already crawling child, the now dead girl who will never crawl again, Baby Suggs tries to take the bloody child from Sethe's arms so that she may nourish her living infant, and that is what this entire struggle has been about for her; feeding and loving and nurturing her children. She ends up aiming her bloody nipple at the baby's mouth, feeding Denver through her sister's blood.

Sethe has broken the law by destroying the white man's possessions, and she must surrender to the forces of law and order. The only thing left to her now is to look. And so, she stares, she places her dread Medusa gaze on the abject men who come in quadruple to recapture this poor woman who has the marvelous ability to multiply her own family. Facing Schoolteacher, she "looked him dead in the eye, she had something in her arms that stopped him in his tracks" and made him step back. "I stopped him… I took and put my babies where they'd be safe," she tells Paul D (Morrison 193). She returns her dread gaze onto the man who attempts to terrorize her, while she herself is beyond all terror, beyond life and death, in a position where her awful maternal love has transported her beyond this world onto another plane. All that Schoolteacher can see is little nigger-boy eyes, little nigger-girl eyes, nigger-baby eyes. "But the worst ones were those of the nigger woman who looked like she didn't have any. Since the whites in them had disappeared and since they were as black as her skin, she looked blind" (Morrison 177). He gives up in despair of any financial gain from this situation, leaving the sheriff to exercise the law against this outlaw woman. But the sheriff can do nothing, since they are petrified under Sethe's gaze, and they "all might have remained that way, frozen till Thursday" (178), until one of the boys on the floor sighs, which releases the sheriff so that he can arrest Sethe. Thus, Sethe's dread Medusa gaze deflects the appropriating male gaze, preventing these men from stealing her children from her. They cannot outface her petrifying stare despite all their cruelty against her. Frozen before her, they remain unable to resist her look, unable to move, until the spell is broken and they are released into movement again. She defies them all and escapes their laws, albeit at a very terrible price in her own flesh and blood.

While men have ravished, beheaded, and made Medusa monstrous, she retains a tremendous force for women. Alice Walker in her novel, *The Temple of My Familiar*, describes divine female power against male denigration. Her title refers to the 'familiar' or bird of life, which is destroyed by ignorance. This bird struggling out from imprisonment and volcanically erupting from being crushed underfoot, bursts into the open air, and finally flies away, instead leaving the oppressor destroyed by its loss (Walker 118-20). Emblematic of Medusa's position, this shows women as indefatigable even as they are crushed, Phoenix-like rising from the ashes of their destruction. Walker describes "the severed head of Medusa, her snakelike locks of hair presented as real snakes—everywhere in Africa a symbol of fertility and wisdom" of this Goddess; "the Great Mother, Creator of All, Protector of All, the Keeper of the Earth. *The* Goddess" (Walker 269). But "the white male world of Greece decapitated and destroyed the black female Goddess/Mother tradition and culture of Africa" (271), bringing them under the heel of patriarchy in raping Africa (Walker 148). Robert Graves states the political suppression of goddess and Medusa myths thus: "The Hellenes overran the goddess's chief shrines, stripped her priestesses of their Gorgon masks, and took possession of the sacred horses" (Graves 17).

Walker describes the fate of many thousands sold into slavery because of their ancient veneration of the mother, unacceptable to the Mohametans, who enforced great suffering and torture by selling mothers into slavery (Walker 63). The Moors who loved the Mother had to "flee the religious dictatorship of Islam" (197) into Spain. Yet the Black Madonna is venerated throughout France and Poland: "Our Black Lady, the Great Mother of All—Mother Africa" (Walker 198), and even God is rumoured to have had a Mother (Walker 249). The Inquisitors asserted that blacks and women were both of the devil, and witches, although the word witch originally meant healers, and such 'witches' brought children into the world, cured the sick, and laid out the dead when all was past; but their power over life was resented and refused (Walker 198), and such women were burned. When men determined themselves to be the creators, they raided the women's temples in their sacred groves of trees, dragging women and children out and forcing them into marriage with male-dominated tribes, enabling women to be owned like chattel, alongside "cattle or hunting dogs," "dethroning women" (64). Walker tells how the ultimate, once unthinkable curse against "Africa/Mother/Goddess—motherfucker—is still in the language" (64). Invaders stripped these people and hacked off their hair, packing them onto slave boats to cross the ocean, branding them as things and violating them physically and sexually, leaving them with the sole resource of the mother's breast milk, which offered their only comfort through those terrible crossings and desecrations.

The Medusa head was once placed on temples, shields, sarcophagi, as well as on more mundane doorways and ovens, as a protective, apotropaic force to protect the site with her stare. The gaze which petrifies, destroying any who dare to approach, is also a protective force that turns away evil attack, operating as an apotropaic force in "literally warding off or turning away the evils it embodies," shielding Medusa's sacred sites, with terror "used to drive out terror" (Garber and Vickers 2). Her gaze turned back against the aggressor thus becomes apotropaic, reverting or turning back the danger and protectively asserting her 'evil eye' against attack. Jean Paul Sartre states that petrification "by the Other's look is the profound meaning of the myth of Medusa" (Sartre 430), Medusa's returning look her archetypal expression. This apotropaic force of the look turned against the Other is supremely shown on the Medusa pediment of the Temple of Corfu.[162] This magnificent statue shows Medusa with her children on either side of her, snakes in her hair and at her waist, as a protective force accessible to those who appeal to her.

Margaret Atwood's *Cat's Eye* presents a fascinating reflection of Medusa's apotropaic gaze by showing the redemptive and divine force of Medusa operating as an evil eye in returning her protective gaze against the other; my writing "Medusa as Female Eye or Icon" shows this divine force saving the young Elaine. The narrator Elaine in Atwood's *Cat's Eye* describes her blue cat's eye marble as the central symbol of this novel, representing her "life entire" (Atwood 420). She uses this blue marble as a talisman to protect herself against the ruthless onslaught of her three putative friends who relentlessly taunt and persecute her, feeling the power of this blue 'evil eye' in her red plastic purse as a force protecting her under

---

[162] See page 38.

duress. She once picks up a picture of the Virgin Mary, "Our Lady of Perpetual Help" on the street, with her halo and crown, her red heart exposed outside her chest. Although she drops the picture immediately in her fear of Cordelia's reproach, she desperately decides to pray to the Virgin Mary. In wordless prayer she sees the Virgin's face surrounded with blue, and is reassured that it is "the heart all right. It looks like my red plastic purse" (Atwood 197). The child of atheist parents, Elaine has scant insight into religious symbolism, and her protestant friends' belief offers her no support in troubled times, instead subjecting her to an implacable force. Yet even as she can scarcely take a proper look at the Madonna's picture under Cordelia's scrutiny, she rebelliously determines to appeal to her.

Cordelia tauntingly drives Elaine down into the icy cold water of the ravine that has seeped through the bodies of the dead in the adjacent cemetery, and she deserts her immersed in this icy water, leaving her there to freeze to death. Elaine gives herself up to the frozen water, listening to the *"hush"* (202) sounds in the snow, reverberating as if the dead people are coming to get her, the tears running down her face because of her frozen hands and feet, desperate about returning back home. Surrendering to her position, she lies back and looks up at the sky, becoming weightless and beyond pain. Then she catches sight of someone on the bridge glowing above her, apparently with rays coming out of her head. Hearing a voice talking to her, and struggling to open her eyes, she sees a woman melting through the bridge, walking toward her as if through air. This woman holds out her arms sympathetically, making Elaine feel "a surge of happiness" (203) as she sees the woman's heart visibly glowing within her. She feels herself folded within her warm embrace, as the woman tells her: *"You can go home now... It will be all right. Go home"* (203). Elaine recognizes her as the Virgin Mary, walking through air and saving her from death by freezing. Her dress, more black than blue, her heart bleeding for Elaine, she clearly "didn't want me freezing in the snow. She is still with me, invisible, wrapping me in warmth and painlessness, she has heard me after all," (204) Elaine observes. She manages to climb up the path toward her mother who is running to save her. As her mother embraces her, the Virgin leaves her, and the "pain and cold shoot back" (205) into her. In this extreme situation, this vision of the Madonna saves Elaine from certain death by operating as a Medusa evil eye, giving her the strength to rise above her fatal position. Sue Monk Kidd in *The Secret Life of Bees* presents the protective black Mary, Our Lady of Chains, as "the voice in you that said, 'No, I will not bow down to this'" (Kidd 357), enabling those who trust her to break free of oppression.

From this point on in her life, Elaine finds the strength that she had previously lacked to reject her friends' persecution, accessing the dynamism of the divine power whose exposed heart operates as an apotropaic Medusa evil eye in saving her, approaching her through the air. Now Elaine is able to defy persecution by stepping out into the air herself and walking away from her mates, knowing that the air will support her, and miraculously it does. She does not need to obey her bullying friends; she has actually never had to, and now she is strong enough to evade their taunts and distance herself from them. Later she finds herself able to revert her own power against Cordelia and subject her to abuse, exerting an almost fatal power over her. From this point on, it is Cordelia who goes crazy and enters a lunatic asylum, with Elaine retaining the power in her own hands.

The Medusa gaze is illustrated in Angela Carter's tale, "The Bloody Chamber" in the collection of the same name. Here, Carter refers to the mother as a Medusa force who wields her petrifying, apotropaic maternal gaze against the usurping male. She returns her protective look against the man who dares to appropriate her daughter for his own evil desires. Carter presents a bestially savage aristocrat who marries and carries off his brides to his isolated castle set in the sea. Coming from a line of bloody and butcherous autocrats, his ancestor had beheaded the beautiful wife of the blacksmith and then pulled her head out of a bag before him, exhibiting this "genus, brunette" (Carter 135). The last in a line of innocent victims, in the Bluebeard tradition, his newest wife discovers the corpses of his three previous wives in his subterraneous torture chamber, the blood still dripping from the Iron Maiden with its impaling spikes, beside the open catafalque and the decapitated skull. The terrified girl, realizing she is the next victim of this predator, drops her key in the fresh blood. She is thus incriminated with Eve's sin of having penetrated his deadly secret, as well as her Eve-like disobedience against this god-like man with his all-seeing eye, observing through the opal ring he leaves behind with her, which he assumes will serve him to purchase a dozen more wives after her death. Surrounded with his possessions, she is free to play with them, make paper boats of his stocks and shares, as long as she does not penetrate his ghastly secret. But he is absolutely sure this is what she is doomed to do and is already on his way back to execute his sentence upon this innocent girl who has uncovered his savagery. Her sole crime—other than knowing his crime, is to have been betrayed into marrying his extraordinary wealth and carnal knowledge, after an impoverished life of hardship where her mother sold her wedding ring to pay for her daughter's piano lessons.

The girl had previously telephoned her mother, bursting into tears from apparent joy while relating her splendid gold bath taps with turquoise blue 'evil eyes,' which her mother intuits as a subliminal cry for help, empathetically alerting her to her daughter's dire situation. These operate as evil eyes in informing her mother (who had never heard her daughter cry for joy before) that something is unearthly wrong in this marquis' haunted castle, and she sets off by train and on horseback to vindicate her innocent child. The climactic scene occurs as the mother arrives with the girl facing death for her Eve-like crime of knowing. The girl and sympathetic blind piano tuner run to unfasten the gate to her mother's pounding and battering, while the marquis stands with his sword raised to execute her, just as Perseus beheaded Medusa at the ends of the world. The mother bursts through the gate with her gun that once saved a village from a ravenous tiger, and was wielded against

Chinese pirates, defending her child like a Fury or Erinyes. The girl relates that miraculously the marquis' "blade did *not* descend, the necklace did *not* sever, my head did *not* roll… the beast wavered in his stroke" (Carter 142). He stands helpless before this Medusa onslaught against him, petrified through the powerful maternal gaze: "My husband stood stock still, as if she had been Medusa, the sword still raised over his head as in those clockwork tableaux of Bluebeard that you see in glass cases at fairs" (142). The mother's powerful Medusa gaze freezes the usurping male into stone, enabling her to shoot this brutal man in the head and release her daughter. The apotropaic force of the Medusa mother thus returns her redemptive gaze against the destructive enemy.

These various accounts present the stunning Medusa as an inspiration for women, as these characters access Medusa's power in their direst need. Toni Morrison shows a woman in the abject position of a slave mother. With precious little she can do beside self-destruction; her Medusa gaze bears her up and beats off the attacks of those around her who are disabled by her remorseless look. Angela Carter presents the empathetically protective mother deflecting the usurping male force in rescuing her daughter, rewriting the fairy tale ending with her victorious apotropaic Medusa gaze. Margaret Atwood similarly shows her character Elaine grasping the maternal and divine vision that beams strength to her through her protective heart. Her 'evil eye' marble becomes the maternal force of the Madonna here operating as a Medusa talisman, saving Elaine and enabling her to rise above passive somnolence and grasp her life in her own hands. These women appropriate Medusa's stunning support of the victim, returning their gaze against violators and saving themselves and those whom they love.

REFERENCES:

Alban, Gillian M. E. "The Serpent Goddess Melusine: From Cursed Snake to Mary's Shield." *The Survival of Myth: Innovation, Singularity and Alterity*. Newcastle upon Tyne: Cambridge Scholars Publishing, 2010.

Alban, Gillian M. E. "Medusa as Female Eye or Icon in Atwood, Murdoch, Carter, and Plath." *Mosaic* 46.4, 2013, 163-182.

Alban, Gillian M. E. The Medusa Gaze in Contemporary Women's Fiction: Petrifying, Maternal and Redemptive. Newcastle upon Tyne: Cambridge Scholars Publishing, 2017.

Atwood, Margaret. *Cat's Eye*. New York: Bantam Books, 1988.

Baring, Anne and Jules Cashford. *The Myth of the Goddess: Evolution of an Image*. London: Penguin, 1991.

Bowers, Susan R. "Medusa and the Female Gaze." *NWSA Journal*, 2.2, 1990, 217-235.

Carter, Angela. *Burning Your Boats: Collected Short Stories*. London: Vintage, 1996.

Dexter, Miriam Robbins. "The Ferocious and Erotic 'Beautiful' Medusa and the Neolithic Bird and Snake" *Journal of Feminist Studies in Religion*. 26.1, 2010, 25-41.

Graves, Robert. *The Greek Myths*. London: Penguin Books, 1955, 1960.

Kidd, Sue Monk. *The Secret Life of Bees*. London: Headline Book Publishing, 2001.

Lawrence, D. H. *The Rainbow*. Harmondsworth: Penguin Books, 1915, 1949.

Morrison, Toni. *Beloved*. London: Vintage, 1987.

Sartre, Jean Paul. *Being and Nothingness*. London: Methuen, 1943.

Walker, Alice. *The Temple of My Familiar*. London: The Women's Press, 1989.

Kahlo Medusa
Meg Dreyer

Making Amends with Medusa
Dawn Glinski

THE FIXED STAR ALGOL, which is part of the constellation Perseus, and located at 26° in the sign of Taurus, is known as the demon star or Medusa's head. For centuries it has been recognized for being the most evil star out there. Algol is associated with pain, suffering, violence, difficult and emotionally intense experiences, beheadings, accidents to the head, losing one's head (mentally)— and has been historically linked with murderous acts, disastrous events, and anything horrific. People are advised to be cautious when personal planets are transiting over Algol, and when natal planets are within close proximity to her, (conjunction) it is viewed to be an unlucky and troublesome placement.

There are many folks out there who, when discovering that they have a personal planet conjunct this fixed star, get what I refer to as *Algol anxiety*. After learning of this placement, panic sets in, people instantly think that they're doomed and find themselves wondering, "What's going to happen? Or "how will I lose *my* head?!" Learning about this so called "unfortunate placement" doesn't have to be an unpleasant experience; in fact, there could be a life altering lesson that needs to be absorbed, that when mastered, can actually improve your life in ways that weren't possible without her presence.

Let's first start by acknowledging the stigmata of this supposed malefic star. Just as every planet has positive and negative manifestations, the stars, depending on their planetary conjunctions, have a similar light and dark as well. To demonstrate this, let's take Saturn for instance; when describing the positive manifestations of this planet, what are the first words that come to your mind? Is it commitment, structure, maybe discipline? Whatever the words, more than likely, it didn't take much time to think of them. Now let's take a moment and try the same exercise with Algol... coming up with those positive words poses more of a challenge, doesn't it?

I think that as students of astrology (and lovers of astrology), we need to be cognizant of the negative implications that we associate with such *bad boy* stars like Algol, who, over the years, have upheld a notorious reputation for representing all things foreboding and evil. While there's no denying the negative manifestations of Algol and the horrendous things that can stem from it, we need to give this star its fair due here. We've heard all about its dark, but what about its light?

Many of us, particularly those who are newer to astrology, don't realize what Algol can offer in terms of benefits. If we can start to make a conscious effort to think about Medusa in a more productive way, the answers are easier to come by. Trying to view her in a more positive light can free us from the blockage that we've created when dealing with her. This lady has important things to say, yet when we don't listen, we wonder how and why things went awry in the first place. *"Blame it on Medusa, for she's the Goddess of undesirable outcomes!"* I can't speak for others, but simply speaking for myself, I'm not comfortable with this mode of thinking.

For most, having a positive aspect involving Algol in the natal chart is still not enough to put us at ease. The likeness of it is comparable to having a friendship with the famed criminal Charles Manson. Given the choice, I'd rather be his friend than his enemy, but ultimately, neither one would make me feel good. I'd prefer to avoid all contact with him if possible, and I think that's how most of us feel about Algol. We don't want any planets near it for fear that no good could come of it either way.

No matter what planet she sits next to, one shouldn't hyperventilate about the nature of the relationship. The point to consider is that Medusa is summoning you to rise to the challenge, respond to the call of action, and make a positive change that will improve your circumstances or the circumstances of those around you. Knowing the true essence of Medusa's energy can allow us to experience the importance of her presence in our chart. Her location shows us how to deal with extremely difficult situations in life *without* losing our heads.

She teaches us to stand on our own two feet, to stick up for ourselves, to fight for the underdog, and to speak out where injustice is concerned. She is deliberately paired with specific planets for a reason. If she happens to be conjunct with one of your planets, consider yourself an ambassador for the cause. Look for what, (planet) how, (sign) and where (house) you are being called upon to make a difference. To tap into the positive energy of this star you can start by asking yourself the following: What am I passionate about? What do I feel needs to be preserved or protected? What am I an advocate for? Keep in mind, Algol is a FIXED star in the sign of Taurus so she is determined to make a difference somehow, somewhere in your world. With Taurus ruling the throat, her placement will urge you to speak up when something isn't right.

Three words that I associate with Algol are protection, preservation, and prevention. Algol instills a need to protect and preserve things that are sacred and important: physical structures, the physical body, certain values, traditions, and beliefs—and because her placement is so strongly linked with advocacy, it can manifest a strong desire in the native to go above and beyond to prevent someone or something from being victimized.

An Algol/Jupiter native could be someone who fights to get prayer back into schools, while an Algol/Saturn native fights to prevent a historical building from being torn down. An Algol/Mars native could be a self-defense teacher (showing others how to *fight* for themselves), while somewhere out there an Algol/Moon individual is involved in establishing or changing parental rights. Algol brings out the natural born fighter in people. Her relentless passion combined with the grace of Venus gives us the power to take charge and face problems head-on without fear. She makes us comfortable with the uncomfortable.

With Algol in an Earth sign she likes to get results. She says, "Don't *tell* me what you're going to do, DO it!" The rage that she is most notably associated with, when released, can produce great change. She is a great strategist, both cunning and creative.

Donald Trump has Algol conjunct his MC—I found this to be most apparent during his show The Apprentice, where he would scream "you're fired" at those he felt weren't pulling their own weight; he's an advocate for those with a strong work ethic, and his anger is his strength. The political leader and Lord Protector of England, Oliver Cromwell had Algol conjunct with Mercury. He was known for his fierce determination and outspoken nature; his main concern was that his country was ruled *fairly*. Former president John Fitzgerald Kennedy had Algol conjunct Jupiter. He fought for desegregation within schools, pushed for the civil rights legislation, and instilled a belief system in Americans with the tagline "it's not what your country can do for you, but what *you* can do for your country." Folk singer Bob Dylan has Algol conjunct Uranus. He was heavily involved with the Civil Rights Movement and rebelled against the establishment through his music. I can go on and list other well-known people with Algol conjunctions who have been equally productive, but the point I wanted to make was this: There is no shortcut to personal growth; if the process was easy, then we wouldn't refer to it as growing pains—but it does tell us something about our character; and character is built upon struggle. Algol can indicate where we may struggle in life, but if we can embrace the messages that Medusa has for us, we can overcome the struggle—and emerge with a new sense of self, dignity, and strength that we didn't realize we had.

REFERENCES:

The Horror-Scope of Algol – Nick Kollerstrom – Skyscript
Algol Star – The Blinking Demon – Astrology King
Fixed Star Algol – Medusa's head – Darkstarastrology

Snakes Aren't Mean!
Arna Baartz

Illustration from *My Name is Medusa*, a children's book by Glenys Livingstone Ph.D.

Mother Medusa

Elizabeth Oakes, Ph.D.

Mother Medusa,
nightmare mother,
the archetypal I-don't-want-to-be-like-my-mother mother,
ball-breaker mother,
mother who takes no shit

mother with hair of snakes,
eyes of newt,
breasts of granite,
tongue of alley cat,
heart like rolling tide in storm

your raging spirit like a
hurricane,
tornado,
tsunami,
earthquake,
thunderstorm,
all contained in the wind tunnel of your throat

you scare those who shutter
the windows at a drop of rain,
who always smile into the mirror,
who fear the fire that reflects
in your Medusa eyes
and in their eyes

mother Medusa,
they told us you were a monster, a witch, a hag,
then they called us that

mother Medusa,
we interpret it another way –
a "you-call-me-bitch-like-it's-a-bad-thing" way

O mother Medusa,
we welcome you into this century,
we will not avert our eyes from you again,
we know we will not be turned to stone

we know the stone is our lost heart

Originally appeared in *Matrix of the Mothers*.

The Medusa Imaginal
Pegi Eyers

WHEN I PUT ON MY PAPER MEDUSA MASK,[163] my serpent jewellery and snakeskin robes, I embody an ancient feminine force of resistance, seeking to shut down all that is harmful to life, like imperialist patriarchies and other walls of division. If Medusa's talents are to freeze male violence and warfare and stop the androcracy in its tracks, then her converse role as nurturer, rewilder and sustainer of the living green world must equally be in play. Undulating across the land like magnetic lines of earth-emergent serpentine delight, the Medusa mythos inspires us to rage against the machine, and to never, ever forget our bond to the Ancestral Mothers and their sacred legacy of love. **Strong in my own Medusa energy,** embodying the hard and the soft, the holding and the letting go, I can't imagine a more empowering role model for women. May you know the blessings of Medusa's fury!

---

[163] Christos Kondeatis, *Masks: Ten Amazing Masks to Assemble and Wear*, Genesis Productions, 1987.

Medusa Mask 1

Medusa Mask 2

Re-visioning Medusa: A Personal Odyssey
Sara Wright

ALL THROUGH MY CHILDHOOD, a self-portrait painted by my mother hung above my parents' bed. I was fascinated by this image of the stern face of my very beautiful mother with her long wavy chestnut hair. In the painting, my mother's body was buried in the sand. Behind her, churning waves cascaded onto the shore. A blue sky was visible. A few seashells were scattered around and a large shiny green beetle was crawling over the sand. This image of my mother with her long curly hair seemed quite frightening to me. It was as if this painting held a key—but to what?

I can remember playing at the seashore. My father would dig holes and bury both his children up to their necks in the warm sand that also held us fast...

I had one reoccurring childhood nightmare of waking up and not being able to breathe.

I first heard the word Medusa when my mother mentioned her in relationship to herself in jest. *Did I ask about her?* My memory is silent on these two points, but I knew Medusa's hair was writhing with snakes and that she was screaming. I also knew my mother was terrified of snakes. Because my mother was an artist, it is possible that I saw an image of Medusa in one of her art books (when I looked for images for this essay one seemed too familiar).

I had another reoccurring childhood dream. My mother and I were locked in a bathroom. There were snakes crawling all over the floor. My mother jumped on the toilet seat and I was left alone on the floor with the snakes. I awakened screaming...

Once, while walking in the woods, a garter snake slithered across the path separating my mother and me. When I screeched in terror my mother turned on me viciously. Stunned and humiliated, I endured her tirade, hopelessly confused…

When my little brother encouraged me to touch a snake in his terrarium one day, I agreed. I was amazed at how silky the snake's skin felt. This animal was quite beautiful with his red tongue and golden eyes and the snake seemed unafraid and friendly. After this encounter my fear of snakes vanished…

As an adolescent I started to call myself Medusa.

Any time I acted out—losing my temper—I berated myself.

In time, self-loathing became the mask I wore.

I hated my body.

Did I dismiss my body because my mother had buried hers below the threshold of awareness?

I told anyone who would listen that I was "a lousy carbon copy of my mother" because that was how I saw myself. No one challenged me on this remark except my grandmother who told me once that she didn't understand why my mother treated me the way she did… My grandmother intercepted my mother, but never confronted her openly.

In my early 20's my brother's suicide and my grandmother's death severed me from any roots I might have had to the earth and any *relationships,* including those with my children; I entered the dead years.

I couldn't leave the house.

For my 39th birthday I bought myself a gold serpent ring. When I placed the ring on my left hand (on my ring finger) I intuited with amazement that on some level I was "marrying" myself. I also thought of my mother (who was still afraid of snakes) and experienced a peculiar sense of power and freedom. The hair on my arms prickled and I shivered involuntarily. I didn't know what my body was specifically trying to convey, but I believed I was prepared to journey into the unknown.

One day I walked to the little beach down the road from my house and discovered a clay deposit in the river. Where had it come from? It was a lovely summer afternoon as I sat down in the wet sand. I scooped up a ball of the dove gray clay and began shaping it into what would become the very first of many bird woman sculptures. This bird woman had a serpent that spiraled around her body. Experiencing an eerie sense of disbelief, I took her home wondering what this image might mean. I had never worked with clay before.

Soon I would be steeped in mythology and the world of the Great Goddess. Shaped by the scholarship of Marija Gimbutas—and fascinated by her powerful images of snakes and women—the serpent came to life as an aspect of self and I had married him.

I went camping and re-discovered the forest, and moved to the mountains where I began to write…

I kept shallow clay bowls full of water for the snakes around my house. I kept their skins after they shed them in the wood pile.

When I dreamed about two iridescent blue snakes, my dog died. I came to understand that snakes had both a powerful positive and negative charge, and that both involved the *body*. I recognized that it was important to be aware of this holy aspect of snakes because they embodied life and death in the Great Round. My respect for all snakes deepened.

Last August I came to Northern New Mexico and became acquainted with Avanyu, the indigenous Tewa name for the horned serpent that is pecked into many rocks as a petroglyph. Avanyu, the Spirit of Water and Life lives in Si-pa-pu (the underworld) and is a powerful supernatural being for the Tewa. He is fierce and unpredictable, presiding over endings and beginnings. He represents change, transition, and transformations that literally occur in the body as it sheds another skin.

Recently, I was given a small shiny black Tewa pot with Avanyu's image carved into its micacious clay surface. A spirit pot. Once again, I have become enamored by a serpent!

As I began this essay, I wondered how Avanyu's serpentine aspect might relate to my writing about Medusa. I certainly believe he is highlighting the importance of needing to live through the truth of my body.

When I first began researching the myth, I was appalled by my own ignorance of Medusa. I had never studied this tragic story because I thought I knew who Medusa was.

I learned that she was one of three sisters, a *Daughter of Earth and Sea* who "lived at the world's edge," the only sister that was mortal. Medusa became one of Athena's priestesses, dedicating her life to the goddess. After Medusa broke her vows and was raped by Poseidon, Athena cursed her, forcing her into a demonic role. The mask of fury that Medusa wore was not one she chose, I realized with a shock. It was thrust upon her by Athena who betrayed her, and who also saw to it that Medusa was shunned and cast out. Eventually Medusa escaped her mortal misery through death. Athena then took Medusa's head, attached and wore it on her shield. Athena could now deflect the powers of female rage/hatred in her mind, if not in her body.

Medusa was a woman who was victimized and twice betrayed by a goddess she adored.

I now identify with Medusa's rage and grief, owning her as a part of me. I had already learned that my rage and grief toward my mother needed to be expressed in a healthy way by holding her accountable for her actions even after her death—but I had never associated Medusa with this process until I read the myth. It's critical to note that I had also learned that the "monstrous" aspect of Medusa can be *removed* at will as long as a woman has developed some conscious awareness and an ability to *contain* and release negative feelings and emotions by living through her *body*.

I also intuited that Athena and Medusa were two aspects of the same figure. One lived through intellect, the other lived through feeling, the very pattern that dominated the relationship between my mother and me. Throughout my life people often told me that my mother envied me, but I could never understand why. I now believe that the core of the issue between Athena and Medusa was Athena's *envy*. Athena "wins" by acquiring power over her victim. Athena does not develop the powers of self-reflection; instead, she persecutes her servant. *Medusa's head becomes an aspect of Athena that is associated with the power to annihilate, to turn others to stone, but this power lacks a body so it remains vulnerable.* My mother drank and attacked her daughter routinely. Drunk or sober, she never said she was sorry. As an adult I was terrified of her rages.

Athena is a goddess of war; she is allied with patriarchal "power over" and the masculine *ideal* of wisdom. She was born from Zeus's neck, not through a woman's body—an unholy birth if there ever was one. My mother was a daughter of intellect who *demanded* absolute allegiance from her daughter and ridiculed all feelings.

The conflict between Athena/Medusa has taught me about the problem of female envy and woman hatred. Medusa was abused and abandoned. As an outcast, Medusa died in a state of terrible despair. Her terrifying loneliness is evident in the images of Medusa that reveal female *misery*, not the face of female evil. My mother refused to see me for the last twelve years of her life. (She had both of my children working for her as henchmen and demanded absolute loyalty from them as well.) When she died at 86 years old, I was relieved. A dream told me that my mother would have lived longer if she had made peace with the daughter she rejected.

I would argue that the snakes in Medusa's hair are symbolic representations of woman's power. Women and serpents have a long history together, one that stretches back to Neolithic times when serpents were seen as wisdom figures, embodying the life force within women, men, and in nature. Like the Minoan Snake goddess—or Avanyu, who speaks to the power of the body and contains both life and death aspects in one serpentine figure— Medusa's writhing serpents reveal that the potential for wisdom is present in woman's intellect. However, we as women must live in our bodies in order to express this potential.

Today I understand why I feared my mother so much as a child and as an adult. She was cut away from her body—a Medusa waiting in the wings to emerge... As a child and a woman who was carrying feelings for both mother and daughter, it was impossible for me to stand up to this woman. Instead, I projected my overwhelming fear and unconscious anger onto myself and continued to adore my mother until her betrayals became intolerable.

Unlike my mother, I gradually, painfully, learned how to own my negative feelings, to contain them and release them from the body

I once despised. I also learned that no matter what I did I could never please my mother because she remained a male-identified woman until her death, choosing any male figure over her own daughter. Like many male-identified women, my mother was a woman hater.

Today I feel great compassion for the mythical Medusa, for the woman in myself, and for any woman who has to deal with a woman-hating mother.

I am finishing this essay on the day after the Women's March on Washington (and everywhere else around the world). The massive worldwide protest highlights how effective women's anger/rage can be when it is embodied and mobilized into a peaceful collective movement that has at its core the belief that women, and the sensible/sensitive men that support them, will not put up with more abuse—verbal or physical. We say NO to giving up our hard won rights. We say NO to the destruction of the planet and its non-human species, to misogyny, to rape, to privileging one group over another, to restricting reproductive rights, to building stupid walls, to isolating one group of individuals from another. We embody Medusa's rage with conscious awareness and begin to fight back. This misogynist who became president partly because 53 percent of white women voted him in must be stopped. First, the proliferation of women hatred and other hatred that abounds in this country needs to be owned, and then huge numbers need to take to the streets to protest. The greatest challenge is to keep up the momentum. Women must gaze with the eyes of Medusa on the monster lurking behind the doors of the Oval Office. Women and men everywhere must turn him to stone.

Today, the portrait of my mother hangs in my oldest son's house, and the last time I saw it a number of years ago, I had an illumination. This was where the painting belonged. I believed then and now that my son had chosen it unconsciously because his lifetime treatment of me mirrors that of his maternal grandmother.

I conclude this essay with a personal note on serpents. I believe that the serpent saved my life because by "marrying" him I opened the door to the unconscious waters, the wisdom of my body, my dreams and to the possibility of living my life authentically. My greatest challenge, then as now, is to stay in this body when I am in deep distress. But I will never make a conscious choice, as my mother once did, to bury my body in the sand.

Adorations For Medusa
Rev. Angela Kunschmann

I hear the hissing before I see you
Such a lovely face
Framed by slender creatures
Snapping and hissing
Protecting you
Readying you for transition
A transition into power
That special womanly power

I see your beauty where others see anger
An otherworldy beauty that is a wonder to behold
I see your beauty in your strength
In your passion
In that special womanly power
I do not turn to stone
Like men who freeze in the presence of womanly strength
I do not run in fear
Like men who cannot appreciate your power
I do not arm myself
Like men who fear what they cannot control

Dear, sweet Medusa
May I find my own creatures to protect me
To ready me for transition
To step into my own womanly power.
May I continue to share the glories of You.

Museo Massimo
Susan Hawthorne

Photo taken at an exhibition held in the Museo Massimo,
Rome in early 2014.

Medusa and Athena:
Ancient Allies in Healing Women's Trauma
Laura Shannon

'Rather than being a bleeding image of female disempowerment, Medusa may be read as... one of the most ancient European symbols of women's spiritual abilities... [and] an empowering image of feminine potential.'[164]

Medusa is familiar to many as a symbol of women's rage. Many feminists see their own rage reflected in the image of Medusa, 'female fury personified.'[165] With her fearsome countenance framed with snakes, able to paralyse with a glance, it is true that Medusa is terrible, terrifying—but she is also terrified. Her face, frozen in an openmouthed scream, eyes wide, teeth bared, is the primal, primate mask of fear.[166] This gut-wrenching image is an eloquent expression of women's rage, but also, I suggest, of women's trauma. In this short essay, I suggest that Medusa, Athena and Metis—goddesses of wisdom, healing, and protection—can offer valuable support to those on the journey of healing from trauma, but first we must look beyond patriarchal stereotypes which denigrate these powerful goddesses. Ultimately, we are invited to hold our fear, rage and trauma in a place of love and compassion, for ourselves and others, so that we can be protected, instead of paralyzed.

Hillman states that 'myths live vividly in our symptoms,' and Keller responds, 'symptoms live vividly in our myths.'[167] Paralysis, rage

---

[164] Monaghan 1994:244.
[165] Culpepper 1986:239.
[166] Van der Kolk 2014:85.
[167] Hillman 1979:23, Keller 1986:51.

and disembodiment, three main elements of the Medusa story, are classic symptoms of post-traumatic stress disorder (PTSD).

According to trauma healing expert Bessel van der Kolk, numbing, freezing, and immobilization are common responses to trauma, particularly sexual trauma. As well as causing a sense of being emotionally shut down, long-term trauma held in the body can result in 'stiff,' 'rigid,' or 'stilted' movement, posture, and expression, resembling paralysis. Trauma can also erode key social skills of self-control and self-regulation, causing the uncontrollable rage characteristic of PTSD. The brutal separation of head from body, a third element of Medusa's story, may reflect the dissociation, fragmentation, and disconnection from the body also typical of the post-traumatic state.[168]

For people with PTSD, trauma can seem to 'go on forever,'[169] as flashbacks may occur at any time in which the trauma is re-experienced as if it were actually happening. In this way the original trauma becomes eternal, an inner silent scream held in the body, an agony which perhaps to the sufferer feels not unlike Medusa's countenance of rage and pain. (Perhaps Medusa's head illustrates this state, the hissing, writhing snakes like neural pathways out of control.)

Freud famously saw the 'horror' of Medusa's head as a symbol of male castration, but the original trauma in the Medusa story is not castration but rape. Most scholars and historians dismiss Poseidon's rape of Medusa as an insignificant detail, merely one among so many rapes of mortal, immortal and semi-divine women committed by male gods. However, myths which glorify rape as a strategy 'to enact the principle of domination by means of sex' are comparatively recent, becoming widespread in Attica around the 5th century BCE.[170]

---

[168] Van der Kolk 2014:14, 20, 26, 12, 10, 19, 66.
[169] Van der Kolk 2014:70.
[170] Keuls 1985:47-49.

It is likely that myths celebrating rape reflect a devastating historical shift in cultural values, the change from a society based on equality and partnership to a hierarchical structure based on unequal distribution of resources and the need to control women's sexuality.[171] Joseph Campbell describes the myth of Perseus and Medusa as reflecting 'an actual historic rupture, a sort of sociological trauma' which occurred in the early thirteenth century B.C.E.[172] The myth may refer to the overrunning of the peaceful, sedentary, matrifocal and most likely matrilineal early civilizations of Old Europe by patriarchal warlike Indo-European invaders.[173]

Miriam Robbins Dexter points out that '[t]he slaying of the demon, or demonized figure, may be a motif particular to patriarchal societies.'[174] In the epic of Gilgamesh, the hero kills the demon Humbaba, whose severed head may serve as a prototype for that of Medusa. This image may also reflect the trauma of women raped during war.

Carol P. Christ sees Classical Greek images of Perseus holding the severed head of Medusa as a 'celebration of the conquest of the civilization of the Goddess'—the shift to a patriarchal culture of war.[175] This patriarchal system is described by Christ as arising at 'the intersection of the control of women, private property, and war—which sanctions and celebrates violence, conquest, rape, looting, exploitation of resources, and the taking of slaves.' It is 'a system of domination enforced through violence and the threat of violence' ... 'in which men dominate women through the control of

---

[171] Gimbutas 1991, Eisler 1987, Haarmann 2014.
[172] Campbell 2011:152.
[173] This has been discussed and described by Marija Gimbutas (1991), Riane Eisler (1987), Joan Marler (2002:15-16), Harald Haarmann (2014), Carol P. Christ (2016) and others.
[174] Dexter 2010:34, note 43.
[175] Christ 2015.

female sexuality with the intent of passing property to male heirs.'[176]

As Christ points out, rape has been recorded as a tool of war since the time of Homer's Iliad as well as in the Hebrew Bible.[177] War itself, in the words of Anne Baring, is a rape of the soul, 'a terrible wound... that can never heal because of the legacy of the trauma and memories it leaves behind, not only with the living but with the dead.'[178] The Medusa myth embodies this tragedy: Medusa is both enraged and outraged. Rape is an outrage. Her eternal open-mouthed silent scream reveals the anguish not only of one individual survivor of rape, but of all those subjected to the horror of rape as a war crime and a technique to enforce norms of patriarchy—a method still in use today.

The name Medusa means 'sovereign female wisdom,' 'guardian/protectress,' 'the one who knows' or 'the one who rules.' It derives from the same Indo-European root as the Sanskrit Medha and the Greek Metis, meaning 'wisdom' and 'intelligence.'[179] Metis, 'the clever one,' is Athena's mother. Corretti identifies Athena, Metis, and Medusa as aspects of an ancient triple Goddess corresponding respectively to the new, full, and dark phases of the moon.[180] All three are Goddesses of wisdom, protection, and healing.

Athena and Medusa are particularly linked: indeed, one may have been an aspect of the other, 'two indissociable aspects of the same sacred power.'[181] Their many common elements include snakes, wings, a formidable appearance, fierce eyes and powerful gaze. The

---

[176] Christ 2016:216. When I refer to patriarchy in this paper, I am using Christ's definition.
[177] Christ 2016:216, 219, 220.
[178] Baring 2013, p 295-6.
[179] Garcia 2013; Monaghan 1994:234; Marler 2002:17, 25; Kerenyi 1951:118. Keller (1986:57) affirms that 'Metis and Medusa are one.' See also: https://en.wiktionary.org/wiki/μέδω.
[180] Corretti 2015:5.
[181] Monaghan 1994:239; Brunel 1996.

serpent, like the Goddess, has been cast as an embodiment of evil in patriarchal retellings; yet as Merlin Stone points out, serpents were 'generally linked to wisdom and prophetic counsel,' associated with 'the female deity' and 'entwined about accounts of oracular revelation... throughout the Near and Middle East.'[182] According to Ovid, the poisonous vipers of the Sahara 'arose from spilt drops of Medusa's blood.'[183] Although this is presented as a further sign of Medusa's horrifying character, the original Berber inhabitants of North Africa—where Herodotus reports that the Medusa myth began—viewed snakes as bringers of luck and portents of joy.[184]

Despite Medusa's fearsome appearance, she herself does not personify evil or demonic forces. According to Miriam Robbins Dexter, Medusa is a manifestation of the Neolithic serpent/bird Goddess of life, death, and regeneration.[185] Jane Harrison explains that the ancient Goddess wore the Gorgon mask to warn the uninitiated away from her rites,[186] most likely mysteries of the great cosmic cycles of heaven and earth. Patricia Monaghan sees the snakelike rays streaming out from Medusa's countenance as a sign of a solar Goddess,[187] while Joan Marler, citing her connection with Hecate, identifies Medusa more with the moon than the sun;[188] either way, Medusa is a heavenly deity ruling over the powers of the cosmos and the rhythms of time.

The Medusa story is just one of many in which, in the words of Annis Pratt, 'the beautiful and powerful women of the pre-Hellenic religions are made to seem horrific and then raped, decapitated or

---

[182] Stone 1976: 199, 200, 209; see also Gimbutas 1989, Dexter 2010 on the snake and the Neolithic Goddess of rebirth.
[183] Metamorphoses 4.622-25, 770.
[184] Herodotus 2.91.6; Musée Berbère 2015:37.
[185] Dexter 2010:33, Gimbutas 1989:206-8.
[186] Harrison 1908:187-8.
[187] Monaghan 1994:237.
[188] Marler 2002:23, note 3.

destroyed.'[189] Just as the ancient goddess Medusa was converted into a monster, Athena's actions in relation to Medusa have also been depicted as monstrous, but this, too, is a relatively recent patriarchal portrayal, and deserves reevaluation.

The portrayal of Athena as antagonist to Medusa first appears in Ovid, as late as the first century CE.[190] In Ovid's version of the story, Athena curses Medusa with a horrifying countenance and snakes for hair, then assists Perseus on his quest to cut off Medusa's head.[191] Athena is depicted as an enemy of women, a traitor to her gender, an impression strengthened by the oft-quoted words put into her mouth by the Classical playwright Aeschylus: 'I am exceedingly of the father...'[192]

But these are later interpretations. Earlier Medusa myths, as related by Homer, Hesiod, Pindar and others, make no mention of enmity from Athena; nor do authors contemporary with Ovid including Strabo.[193] Ovid and Aeschylus exemplify classic patriarchal strategies that blame the victim, set women against one another, and reframe ancient myths to the detriment of powerful females. Athena and Medusa have both been diminished in this way, as has Athena's mother Metis, who has been 'disappeared' from the scene of Athena's birth. But do we really wish to let these great goddesses of wisdom be defined by the authors and artists of patriarchy? Older, pre-patriarchal versions of Athena reveal her deeper nature.

---

[189] Pratt 1978:168, quoted in Monaghan 1994:237.
[190] Metamorphoses, IV. 779ff.
[191] Ovid presents this as Athena punishing Medusa for having been raped by Poseidon in Athena's temple (Metamorphoses IV. 850-8). Earlier versions relate that Medusa was born with serpent locks. See also Rigoglioso 2009:74.
[192] Aeschylus, Eumenides 736-8, in Deacy 2008:17.
[193] Homer, Iliad 5.738 ff; Hesiod, Theogony 275-280; Pindar, Pythian 12.7-22; Strabo, Geography 8.6.21.

Athena was a pre-Greek divinity, honoured by the native Europeans whom the Greeks called Pelasgians, 'neighbours.'[194] Like Medusa, she was originally a great cosmic Goddess of heaven and earth, the deity of life, death and regeneration who was venerated in Old Europe for thousands of years. She is connected by some with the North African Goddess Neith and with the Mesopotamian Inanna, known for her descent to and return from the underworld.[195] Patriarchal portrayals of Athena emphasize her warlike aspect (and there is evidence that her warrior traits were later acquisitions),[196] and some pacifist feminist scholars find Athena problematic for this reason. It is beyond the scope of this paper to attempt to resolve the question of the origin of Athena's warrior nature—Medusa may also have been a woman warrior, perhaps a North African Amazon priestess and queen.[197]

I suggest we continue to look beyond the distortions of patriarchal interpretations and begin to reclaim ancient Goddesses in their original autonomy and power. Miriam Robbins Dexter's conclusions about Medusa could equally apply to Athena:

> '[Medusa] reminds us that we must not take the female "monster" at face value; that we must not only weigh her beneficent against her maleficent attributes but also take into consideration the worldview and sociopolitical stance of the patriarchal cultures which create her, fashioning the demonic female as scapegoat for the benefit and comfort of the male members of their societies.'[198]

A multidisciplinary approach can serve us best, drawing on new scholarship in the fields of classics, archaeology, and linguistics, in combination with an open-ended Jungian approach in which each

---

[194] Haarmann 2014:9.
[195] Deacy 2008:41; Rigoglioso 2010:24.
[196] Deacy 2008:38.
[197] Pausanias 2.21.5; Rigoglioso 2009:71.
[198] Dexter 2010:41.

seeker can find their own sense of meaning in ancient archetypes of the Goddess.

Athena is not only a Goddess of war. She is a complex and polyvalent Goddess with many other qualities—as Goddess of healing, of wisdom, of protection and self-defense, of craft and culture, of the olive tree—which can have great significance for all those healing from trauma. I would like to focus on some of them here, in particular, Athena's aspect as Goddess of protection.

Perseus' part in the Medusa myth ends with him carrying the Gorgon's head to the court of King Polydectes, who had been scheming all along to get Perseus out of the way so he could marry Perseus' mother Danae. When Perseus uses the power of the Gorgon to destroy Polydectes, we see that Athena, in helping him, ultimately has acted to protect Danae from forced marriage and rape.

I suggest that Athena in her armour can be understood as a sign that women can and must be protected. The Goddess herself needs protection, if she is to survive the perils of a patriarchal era. Athena's skills of strategic protection and clever defense are vital to women who—like Athena herself—are prisoners of patriarchy. She is the Goddess of protected spaces: the walled city, the castle, the acropolis, and the women's wisdom and culture contained therein. As guardian and protectress, Athena in antiquity was 'envisaged as a caring and feminine, not to say maternal, figure.'[199]

Athena's helmet may represent the protection of our neural pathways, as mentioned earlier. The experience of trauma affects our ability to think clearly. Therefore the work of healing requires the clear thinking and clear seeing which are also Athena's gifts. The quality of mindfulness, defined by Bessel van der Kolk as the ability 'to hover calmly and objectively over our thoughts, feelings and

---

[199] Deacy 2008: 108.

emotions,'[200] is a key part of recovery and also of Athena's mental power.

The theme of protection manifests when Athena places Medusa's head on her breastplate or aegis, right in the centre of her heart. Medusa's head now becomes the universally powerful apotropaic emblem, the Gorgoneion, placed on shields, walls, houses, temples, roofs, gates and entryways throughout Classical antiquity and even in the present day. I believe this action has profound significance for our theme of healing from trauma.

Great rage needs a great heart to hold it; great trauma needs a great heart to heal it. Athena's many epithets include 'the Great-Hearted' and 'She Who Saves.'[201] By placing Medusa's severed head in the centre of her heart, I suggest that Athena is acting to 'save' Medusa, by containing her rage with love and compassion, so it can be witnessed, honoured and remembered. In the words of Bessel van der Kolk, 'trauma almost invariably involves not being seen, not being recognized, and not being taken into account... sensing, naming, and identifying what is going on inside is the first step to recovery.'[202]

The Gorgoneion in the centre of Athena's heart reminds me of the Buddhist practice of *tonglen*, breathing in and out of the heart centre while holding an awareness of all the hurts and evils of this world. Tonglen is seen as a way to bring the balm of compassion to the worst and deepest wounds inflicted by humanity and is considered an extremely difficult practice. To consciously witness the terrible pain, the collective and individual rage of the betrayed and wounded feminine, simply to hold it in the presence of divine love and compassion, requires tremendous strength and courage.

---

[200] Van der Kolk 2014:62.
[201] Solon 4.3 in Deacy 2008:78; Homeric Hymn to Athena 28:3.
[202] Van der Kolk 2014: 59, 68.

Healing from trauma also requires courage, along with protection, mindfulness, compassion and love. The Sanksrit name Medha, related to Medusa, also has the meaning of 'intellect illuminated by love.'[203] This is exactly the power of mind or mindfulness which can help us heal.

Athena's wisdom is strategic. She is cunning and clever. Her clear sight reveals the simple truth that however justified our anger may be, it serves nothing if we let it destroy us. Anger brings gifts, lessons, protection, power. So, we must not seek to destroy the anger either, but rather welcome it with compassion and place it safely in our hearts where it can protect us.

By placing Medusa's head in her heart, Athena gives Medusa a post-trauma sanctuary in a safe and strong body, and Medusa gives Athena a part of her protective powers. In this way, Athena helps heal the rage, fear and trauma of the Medusa story and transform it into an energy for protection, in the form of the Gorgoneion. The Gorgoneion is a reminder that rage can protect us, by helping us stay alert in the face of potential danger. Medusa has been made into a monster; yet as Catherine Keller points out, the original meaning of the Latin *monstrum* is 'a portent,' connected to *monstrare,* 'to show' and *monere,* 'to warn', from the same root as *remember, remind,* and *mind*.[204] The Gorgoneion shows, warns, helps us remember, and reminds us to be mindful. As Emily Culpepper writes, 'The Gorgon has much vital, literally life-saving information to teach women about anger, rage, power, and the release of the determined aggressiveness sometimes needed for survival.'[205] Medusa and Athena can thus be seen as teachers of life-saving protection and defense.

As well as protection, Athena brings further gifts to the work of healing from trauma. Past trauma can be transformed through

---

[203] https://www.pitarau.com/meaning-of-medha
[204] Keller 1986:50, 90.
[205] Culpepper 1986:241.

'physical experiences that directly contradict the helplessness, rage and collapse that are part of trauma' and which foster a renewed sense of self-mastery. Because trauma tends to be experienced in 'isolated fragments,' treatment particularly needs to engage the entire organism, 'body, mind, and brain.' [206] Athena's domain includes reading and writing, weaving and handicraft: creative skills which help the survivor engage fully in activities which strengthen new neural pathways for pleasure and joy.

Healing from trauma is also facilitated by rhythmic action shared with others, such as music, song and dance.[207] In ancient Athens, Athena was celebrated with choral dance and song,[208] and similar practices can still be witnessed today in traditional women's circle dances of Greece and the Balkans. Through my lifetime of researching these dances *in situ*, I have come to believe these dances provide essential comfort and healing support for women who must live under patriarchal oppression.[209]

The dance circle itself is like Athena's temple, the *polis*, the round enclosure within which the women are safe. To protect the city is to protect the city's women, and this was Athena's special domain: she was the guardian of the sacred space, the temple, the walled city or *polis* within which the women are kept secure.

I believe that traditional circle dances provide a context for women to affirm and transmit pre-patriarchal values, such as the importance of community, mutual support, and shared leadership, within a circular, not a hierarchical structure.[210]

The dances can help us both receive and give the gifts of protection and healing. Bessel van der Kolk affirms that 'our capacity to

---

[206] Van der Kolk 2014:4, 40, 53.
[207] Van der Kolk 2014:333.
[208] Connelly 2007:29-30, 294.
[209] Shannon 2011:144.
[210] Shannon 2016.

destroy one another is matched by our capacity to heal one another,'[211] and this experience of mutual healing is essential to healing from trauma.

The dances also show the importance of connecting with other women in shared rhythmic and joyful movement and connecting with each other as allies instead of enemies. Ultimately, we can learn to have compassion for ourselves, for each other, and for all those affected by the trauma of patriarchy, including the perpetrators.

Women of the world have been quietly screaming a shared scream for thousands of years. A new understanding of the ancient Goddesses, Athena, Metis, and Medusa, can help us realise that we are worthy of protection. Through distorted portrayals by patriarchal authors, all three of these Goddesses have suffered the trauma of 'not being seen, not being recognized, and not being taken into account,' but we can begin to change and heal this now, by seeing and understanding them more deeply in their original fullness and positivity.

Where Medusa's head symbolises the fear, trauma, and uncontrolled rage experienced by those oppressed by patriarchal society, Athena's original aspect of protection and healing can offer an antidote to the disempowerment, collapse and paralysis of the post-traumatic state. In this way Athena and Medusa can transcend the ancient enmity projected upon them by patriarchal authors and renew the alliance which protects and heals.

The Gorgoneion in the aegis gives protection by teaching us not to be afraid of our rage. By witnessing Medusa's head with mindfulness, love and compassion, we can develop compassion for all victims of the trauma inflicted by patriarchy. Ultimately, we hope

---

[211] Van der Kolk 2014:38.

to claim the power of our rage and outrage, and use it to protect and defend all that we hold dear.

REFERENCES:

Aeschylus. Promethus Bound 790-800.

Baring, A. & Cashford, J. 1991. *The Myth of the Goddess: Evolution of an Image*. London: Penguin.

Brunel, P. ed. 1996. *Companion to Literary Myths, Heroes, and Archetypes*. London: Routledge.

Campbell, J. 2011. *Occidental Mythology*. London: Souvenir Press.

Christ, C. P. 2016. 'The Sacred Feminine or Goddess Feminism?' on FeminismAndReligion.com, Jan. 25, 2016.

Christ, C. P. 2016. 'A New Definition of Patriarchy: Control of Women's Sexuality, Private Property, and War' in Feminist Theology 2016, Vol. 24(3) 214–225.

Christ, C. P. 2017. 'This Is How Liberal Democracy Dies: Will We Let It?' on FeminismAndReligion.com, Feb. 6, 2017.

Connelly, J. 2007. *Portrait of a Priestess*. Princeton: Princeton University Press.

Corretti, C. 2015. *Cellini's Perseus and Medusa and the Loggia dei Lanzi*. Leiden: Brill.

Culpepper, E.E. 1986, 2003. 'Gorgons: A Face for Contemporary Women's Rage' in M. Garber and N. Vickers, *The Medusa Reader*. New York: Routledge.

Deacy, S. 2008. *Athena*. London: Routledge.

Dexter, M. R. 2010. 'The Ferocious and the Erotic: "Beautiful" Medusa and the Neolithic Bird and Snake'. Journal of Feminist Studies in Religion, Vol. 26, No. 1, pp. 25-41.

Eisler, R. 1987. *The Chalice and the Blade*. Cambridge, Mass.: Harper & Row.

Garber, M. and Vickers, N. 2003. *The Medusa Reader*. New York: Routledge.

Garcia, B. 2013. 'Medusa,' in Ancient History Encyclopedia (online).

Gimbutas, M. 1989. *The Language of the Goddess*. San Francisco: Harper & Row.

Gimbutas, M. and Marler, J. 1991. *The Civilization of the Goddess*. San Francisco: HarperCollins.

Haarmann, H. 2014. *Roots of Ancient Greek Civilization*. Jefferson, NC: McFarland.

Harrison, J. 1908. *Prolegomena to the Study of Greek Religion.* Cambridge: Cambridge University Press.

Herodotus and Godley, A. D. 1920. *The Histories.* Cambridge, Mass.: Harvard University Press.

Hesiod and Hine, D. 2007. *Works of Hesiod and the Homeric hymns*. Chicago: University of Chicago Press.

Hillman, J. 1979. *The Dream and the Underworld*. New York: Harper and Row.

Homer and Evelyn-White, H. G. 1914. *The Homeric Hymns and Homerica*. Cambridge, MA., Harvard University Press.

Keller, C. 1986. *From a Broken Web*. Boston: Beacon Press.

Kerényi, K. 1951. *The Gods Of The Greeks*. London: Thames and Hudson.

Keuls, E. 1985, 1993. *The Reign of the Phallus*. 2nd ed. Berkeley: University of California Press.

Marler, J. 2002. 'An Archaeomythological Investigation of the Gorgon.' In ReVision 25, no. 1. pp 15-23.

Monaghan, P. 1994. *O Mother Sun!*. Freedom, CA: Crossing Press.

Musée Berbère. 2015. *Exhibition catalogue*. Marrakesh: Editions Jardin Majorelle.

Ovid, More, B. and Brewer, W. 1978. *Ovid's Metamorphoses*. Francestown (NH): M. Jones.

Pausanias and Jones, W. 2002. *Description of Greece*. Cambridge (Mass.): Harvard University Press.

Pindar. *Pythian 12, For Midas of Acragas Flute-Playing Contest*.

Pratt, A. 1978. 'Aunt Jennifer's Tigers: Notes Towards a Preliterary History of Women's Archetypes.' Feminist Studies 4, February 1978. p.168.

Rigoglioso, M. 2009. *The Cult of Divine Birth in Ancient Greece*. New York: Palgrave Macmillan.

Rigoglioso, M. 2010. *Virgin Mother Goddesses of Antiquity*. New York: Palgrave Macmillan.

Shannon, L. 2011. 'Women's Ritual Dances: an Ancient Source of Healing in Our Time' in J. Leseho and S. McMaster, eds., *Dancing on the Earth: Women's Stories of Healing Through Dance*, 1st ed. Forres: Findhorn Press, 138-157.

Shannon, L. 2016. 'Shared Leadership: The Hidden Treasure of Women's Ritual Dance' on FeminismAndReligion.com, Nov. 1, 2016.

Shannon, L. 2017. 'Women with Wings: Right-brain Consciousness and the Learning Process' in A. Voss and S. Wilson (eds.), *Re-enchanting the Academy*. Seattle: Rubedo Press.

Stone, M. 1976, 1978. *When God Was a Woman*. San Diego, Calif.: Harcourt Brace Jovanovich.

Strabo, Jones, H. and Sterrett, J. 2005. *Geography*. Cambridge, Mass.: Harvard University Press.

Tuana, N. 1993. *The Less Noble Sex: Scientific, Religious, and Philosophical Conceptions of Woman's Nature*. Bloomington: Indiana Unviersity Press.

Van der Kolk, B. 2014. *The Body Keeps the Score*. London: Penguin.

Medusa Self-Portrait
Liliana Kleiner, Ph.D.

Re-stor(y)ing Sanity
Trista Hendren

AS A CHILD I WAS TERRIFIED OF MEDUSA. Ironically, I was drawn to and all-but-obsessed with Pegasus, but I did not know the full story of either character or how they were connected. It makes sense to me now that I would be fascinated by the male offspring of the horrible monster I had been taught to believe myself to be (as female)—and the dream of flying away as a (male) creature who could *finally* satisfy the masculine god I seemed to be inherently incapable of pleasing.

Hélène Cixous reminds us that, "To fly/steal is woman's gesture, to steal into language to make it fly."[212] Reading and writing have been my mode of flight since childhood. Sadly, we are living in a world that devalues both in favor of digital imagery, which I'd argue is a virile venue that will wipe us out eventually. One only has to look to the television adaptation of Margaret Atwood's *The Handmaid's Tale* to illustrate what I mean.[213] While I am aware that many enjoy the show, my belief is the original book has been horribly distorted to instead glorify and normalize violence against women. Our only hope as females is to re-story the world and take back our lives.

For those who grew up in fundamentalist churches like I did, this means finding new sexts[214] for ourselves—as well as embracing

---

[212] Cixous, Hélène. *The Book of Promethea Newly Born Woman (Theory and History of Literature)*. Betsy Wing (Translator). University Of Minnesota Press; 1986.

[213] A full analysis is beyond the scope of this paper, however I recommend the following critique: Prose, Francine."Selling Her Suffering," *New York Times Review of Books.* May, 4 2017.

[214] "Let the priests tremble, we're going to show them our sexts!... Wouldn't the worst be, isn't the worst, in truth, that women... only to stop listening to the Sirens (for the Sirens were men) for history to change its meaning?"
Cixous, Hélène. "The Laugh of the Medusa," translated by Paula and Keith Cohen. 1976.

new she-roes—or uncovering the real power behind those who were demonized.

We also have a great deal of "work" to do on ourselves so that we can heal and live contented lives. As Mary Oliver reminds us, "The long work of turning their lives into a celebration is not easy..."[215]

We hear a great deal about toxic masculinity but rarely about toxic femininity, except from men's rights activists. The results of toxic masculinity are painfully obvious in our world. However, I'd like to briefly explore the effects of toxic *femininity*, which silently kills a lot of us.

I'd say I'm still working on expunging this poison from myself almost daily. It lingers primarily in the expectation (of myself) that I am always "nice" to people—which is something I struggle with. There is nothing wrong with being kind—in fact, I think the world needs more of that. However, females are taught to put themselves so far down the ladder that "nice" is a luxury we can no longer afford ourselves.

If I had my way, every young girl would read Toni Morrison's second but lesser known book, *Sula*. Namely because it was life-changing for me in the way I saw myself as female and the possibilities it opened up for me. As Morrison reminds us, "Being good to somebody is just like being mean to somebody. Risky. You don't get nothing for it."[216]

The biggest lie they tell females is that if you are agreeable and play by all the rules, you will somehow be rewarded and protected by the patriarchal confinement you trade your soul for. *Sula* was my first wake-up call that this was just not so.

---

[215] Oliver, Mary. "The Sunflowers." *Blue Iris*. Beacon Press, 2004.
[216] Morrison, Toni. *Sula*. Knopf, 1976.

Sula was in fact, my Pegasus. Her character allowed me to fly away from the virulent male-perspective I had been groomed to believe in.

When I entered counseling (again) in my mid-twenties, my crone counselor asked me to scream out my rage—and beat it out, if possible with the pillows and other items she had assembled in her cozy office.

I couldn't do it.

This was not a new request of me. When I completed a Dale Carnegie course in high school, I received a similar task. But I couldn't do it at 17 either.

It was only after a stalker broke down my front door and violently attacked me—and I spent the next six months in court trying to obtain a permanent stalking order—that I was finally able to begin to release some of that rage.

One night, I threw a glass down in anger—hard—shattering it into a million little pieces. It felt so satisfying, that I quickly broke *all* my glasses, one after another—failing to notice until afterwards that I was barefoot.

Like many women, I bore the brunt of my own anger with small cuts on my feet, the cost of replacing the glasses—and, later, fixing the damage to my floor. For years I told no one about this incident, deeply embarrassed about my loss of control—and more than anything, how *good* it felt.

Like bell hooks, "I was taught as a girl in a patriarchal household that rage was not an appropriate feminine feeling, that it should be not only not be expressed but be eradicated."[217]

---

[217] hooks, bell. *The Will to Change: Men, Masculinity, and Love.* Washington Square Press, 2004.

Because rage is not a viable option for most girls, many of us have to learn how to utilize it effectively so that we don't hurt ourselves in the process of releasing it. Those with the least amount of power are afforded the smallest amount of anger.

This is exactly why we see so little change. For it is precisely this rage that will turn the world upside down and right-side up again.

The anger I was not allowed to feel as a child still sometimes sneaks up on me. But I don't try to hide it or conceal it anymore. I've come to understand the damage this causes in all areas of our lives.

Jane Caputi wrote:

> "Psychic numbing means never having to feel anything. Refusing such anesthetization and unearthing our passions means facing our emotions, especially those that have been the most anathematized, such as rage, female pride, and self-love. In short, it entails embracing monsters. Lesbian novelist Bertha Harris tells it truly: Monsters express what ordinary people cannot: feel. Monsters are emblems of feeling in patriarchy. Monsters represent the quintessence of all that is female, and female enraged. The monster most emblematic of feeling, most communicative of female rage, is the Gorgon. Many people, consumed by fear, simply cannot meet her gaze. Others, steeped in greed, ignorance, fear, and self-loathing, quite frankly want to lose their senses. Rather than look into the Gorgon's all-seeing eye, they turn themselves to stone—that is, they become psychically numb. Yet those of us who are sick of pretending, denying, suppressing, and repressing our knowledge, our emotions, and our powers journey to her island of rock and stone and there face a laughing, welcoming, and gorgeous

> Gorgon. As we do, we turn not to stone, but to sentient flesh, sensual mind, and boiling blood."[218]

I am sick of pretending, suppressing and, most of all—of repressing.

This is something I have thought about incessantly since giving birth to my daughter Helani, who inspired *The Girl God*.

Hélène Cixous wrote, "I want to become a woman I can love. I want to meet women who love themselves, who are alive, who are not debased, overshadowed, wiped out."[219] This has been my #1 priority in raising Helani—who is now 11.

I have tried to provide the sort of childhood for both my children that I did not have. I came at parenthood with the idea that both my children had far more wisdom than I—not because I am inherently *stupid*, but because I am still learning to come back to my center, which was deeply suppressed. I have not only 'allowed' my children to say what they think and feel no-matter-what—but have facilitated those conversations regularly.

When my daughter was about five, she boldly stated that she was a witch. At first this scared me because of my fundamentalist Christian background, but I soon realized—*of course she was a witch!* I was a witch too. We had always been witches—the fear of burning had dried the truth out of us.

> "Dee L R Graham, in her book *Loving To Survive* examines what she calls 'Societal Stockholm Syndrome.' She hypothesizes that what we refer to as 'feminine' traits—submission, compliance, nurturing, etc—are the result of women living in fear for our lives and trying to ingratiate ourselves with our captors—men—in order to improve our

---

[218] Caputi, Jane. *Gossips, Gorgons and Crones: The Fates of the Earth.* Bear & Company, 1993.
[219] Cixous, Hélène. "The Laugh of the Medusa," translated by Paula and Keith Cohen. 1976.

chances of survival. And she suggests that two centuries of witch trials throughout the world created an environment where women learned not only to comply in order to avoid torture and death, but to police themselves and other women in their behaviour.

But seen in this context, our behaviour is not weakness, it is adaptation. It is survival. When they say, 'we are the granddaughters of the witches you weren't able to burn,' they usually ignore the other edge of the sword. The edge that continues to cut into our collective psyche. But in order to resist we must understand what we are up against. We need to realise why it is so hard to demand the respect that we deserve as human beings. We are, after all, the grandaughters of the compliant women who survived."[220]

Growing up in the church, I spent the first 20 years of my life in dreadful fear of hell fires for every minor infraction I committed. I wasted hours every week, on my knees, begging for forgiveness. As Monica Sjöö and Barbara Mor remind us, "In *no* Goddess religion known were people ever depicted on their knees."[221]

We must learn how to clear and heal ourselves on our own terms.

If only someone would have told me when I was a child, as Glenys did in her children's book about Medusa,[222] that I would be constantly shedding skins that didn't fit anymore—*for the rest of my life*—I think I would have had an easier time of it.

Instead, I feared every mistake, certain that my current circumstances defined who I was as a person. It took me four decades to realize that I could simply shed off what didn't work for

---

[220] Meta. "Burn the Witch" *Where the Wild Words Are.* May 8, 2017. https://thewildwords.wordpress.com/2017/05/08/burn-the-witch/
[221] Sjöö, Monica and Mor, Barbara. *The Great Cosmic Mother: Rediscovering the Religion of the Earth.* HarperOne; 2nd edition, 1987.
[222] Livingstone, Glenys. *My Name is Medusa.* Girl God Books, 2016.

me any longer and re-create myself. As Nayyirah Waheed wrote, "where you are. is not who you are.—circumstances"[223]

When we began this anthology, I felt I really didn't have anything to say about Medusa *personally*. That was not true: I was avoiding my own painful truth (again).

After my abusive ex-husband died unexpectedly last November, I released (even more) suppressed anger. My snakes went wild, biting many of the not-so-innocent in their path.

I was raised to suppress—and even hate—the Medusa within me. Letting Her out was *painful*. My oft-straightened wavy hair was now in a messy, silver-streaked mass around me. I had little energy to control even *that* anymore. I became ill with near constant diarrhea and vomiting. After weeks of tests, doctors found a large (benign) tumor blocking my intestines.

Suppressing my truth—and hence, my rage—was literally killing me.

When I went to my first reiki session after my surgery, the practitioner told me, "Your body is trying to kill you. You hold the rage of all the women throughout history in your being. This isn't your burden to carry any longer." At first, I was angry; then I cried for a long time.

I began to think a great deal about Glenys' question at the beginning of this anthology:

> "What might be the consequences of changing our minds sufficiently, so that Medusa can be comprehended as metaphor for Divine Wisdom? Many scholars contend She once was understood this way. What might it mean for our

---

[223] Waheed, Nayyirah. *Salt*. Createspace, 2013.

minds to welcome Her back? Would that alter the way we relate to Earth, to Being?"[224]

Do we dare consider—and then declare—ourselves Holy? Do we understand that our rage is not only justified—but also sanctified? How do we use that anger effectively—so instead of killing *ourselves*, we utilize it to change the dysfunctional world we live in?

It's easy to let the injustices eat at you and fume instead of letting anger burn as a fire, productively. As Maya Angelou wrote, "Bitterness is like cancer. It eats upon the host. But anger is like fire. It burns it all clean."[225]

I remember writing at one point about wanting to use a toilet brush to scrub my insides clean of all that had been done to me.[226] Had I allowed myself the fury I deserved to feel, the fire might have burned those injustices out of me sooner. Perhaps we are still scared to feel the fire after being burned for so many years.

How might we ordain ourselves as *Worthy*—let alone Goddesses, Priestesses and Leaders—rather than the submissive remnants of ourselves that are (somewhat) acceptable in our woman-hating world? Andrea Dworkin's experience of waking up speaks to me as I ponder this:

> "*I did not experience myself or my body as my own.* I did not feel what was being done to me until, many years later, I read Kate Millet's *Sexual Politics*. Something in me moved then, shifted, changed forever. Suddenly I discovered something inside me, to feel what I had felt somewhere but had had no name for, no place for. I began to feel what was being done to me, to experience it, to recognize it, to find

---

[224] Livingstone, Glenys. *PaGaian Cosmology*, p. 66.
[225] Angelou, Maya. Interview with Dave Chappelle. *Iconoclasts*, the Sundance Channel, 2006.
[226] I write more about my journey in my memoir, *Hearts Aren't Made of Glass: My Journey from Princess of Nothing to Goddess of my Own Damned Life.*

the right names for it. I began to know that there was nothing good or romantic or noble in the myths I was living out; that, in fact, the effect of these myths was to deprive me of my bodily integrity, to cripple me creatively, to take me from myself. I began to change in a way so fundamental that there was no longer any place for me in the world—I was no longer a woman as I had been a woman before. I experienced this change as an agony. There was no place for me anywhere in the world. I began to feel anger, rage, bitterness, despair, fury, absolute fury..."[227]

Our hatred of ourselves is not accidental. That is the insidious result of our specific upbringing as girls. We *learn* to despise and abuse ourselves in both blunt and indirect ways—primarily through the religious texts that seep through our societies and, in many cases, our family of origin. In today's capitalistic societies, media does a lot of the work as well. Whatever self-worth is left is often eaten up by incest and/or rape—as was true in my life. It's easy to control females who deeply loathe and distrust themselves.

Our patriarchal brainwashing has thoroughly rinsed out the richness of our beings—even the biological realities of our bodies. Everything is supposed to be bleached. Our body hair removed. Our faces, masked. Our glorious, womanly smells, perfumed over. Our menses, hidden or erased completely. The fullness of our illustrious bellies, sucked in. Our fat, sucked out. The laugh lines on our faces, smoothed over. Our crowns of silver hair—signifying our crone wisdom—dyed back to more youthful (hence, unknowing) variations.

The crone is perhaps hated most of all; but I've noticed with a daughter who is wise beyond her years (or rather, whose wisdom has not been forced out of her) that there is no love lost for smart,

---

[227] Dworkin, Andrea. "First Love," *The Woman Who Lost Her Names: Selected Writings by American Jewish Women*, compiled and edited by Julia Wolf Mazow. Harper & Row Publishers, 1980.

sassy, bossy little girls. It is so much easier to raise our daughters under the patriarchal framework that instills quietness and submission—the same suppression and repression we are so sick of ourselves as grown women.

The world at large favors authoritarian control of females, instilling obedience from birth. I do not want this for my daughter. I don't want her to spend the first 40 years of her life un-taming herself.

As my daughter approaches the oft difficult time leading to menarche, it is often a painful process to allow her snakes to go wild—and, sometimes bite. Particularly when they bite *me*.

This takes an enormous amount of being present—in a world that favors numbing. I have realized my tendency to turn to stone when my daughter lashes out at me; which is the worst response possible for both of us. By not allowing myself to feel her anger (and mine), I stop the healing process for both of us.

I see in my daughter the quiet little girl I grew up as, who was too afraid to ask *any* questions—come back from the dead. I'll happily take those snake bites for that.

What might it mean to raise our daughters so they do not have to waste a lifetime undoing the toxic indoctrination that most of us endured? What if girls were taught from the get-go to trust their inner voice and feelings, rather than to worship at the feet of men's authority? I like Audre Lorde's answer:

> "When we live from within outward, in touch with our inner power, we become responsible to ourselves in the deepest sense. As we recognize our deepest feelings, we give up, of necessity, being satisfied with suffering and self-negation, and the numbness which seems like the only alternative in our society."[228]

---

[228] Lorde, Audre. "Uses of the Erotic: The Erotic as Power." *Sister Outsider:*

So, how do we get there?

I think we must start with ourselves. After all, we can't teach our daughters what we don't know or remember. We must continue to uncover our own HERstory—or steal it back as the radical pirates Mary Daly suggested we become.[229] We must be diligent about re-learning and deprogramming ourselves. As Janie Rezner wrote:

> "Having suffered under patriarchy for the past 5,000 years, it is not easy, as a woman, to reclaim our rage, our 'maternal instinct,' or to even recognize that we have a universal imperative to be outraged, deep in our cells."[230]

We must learn to not be afraid of this rage— in ourselves or our daughters—as it is She who will release us from our chains. Starhawk reminds us that there is another way—if we can only remember it...

> Memory sleeps coiled
> like a snake...
>
> Breathe deep
> Let your breath take you down
>
> Find the way there
> And you will find the way out[231]

Essays and Speeches. Crossing Press, reprint edition, 2007.

[229] "Women who are pirates in a phallocratic society are involved in a complex operation. First it is necessary to plunder–that is, righteously rip off gems of knowledge that the patriarchs have stolen from us. Second, we must smuggle back to other women our plundered treasures."
Daly, Mary. *Gyn/Ecology: The Metaethics of Radical Feminism.* Beacon Press, 1990.

[230] Rezner, Janie. *She Rises: Why Goddess Feminism, Activism, and Spirituality?* Edited by Helen Hye-Sook Hwang and Kaalii Cargill. Mago Books, 2015.

[231] Starhawk, "Unmasked." *Truth or Dare: Encounters with Power, Authority, and Mystery.* Harpercollins, 1988.

May the coils become unraveled and our passions reign unruly. May we take back the lies we have been told about ourselves and re-story the world. May our collective rage restore our sanity, facilitate healing—and finally—bring peace. May we all learn not to fear our own power—*or Medusa's*—but to laugh from the bottom of our bellies with Her. May we teach our daughters to love themselves *deeply*—and may that love serve as a reminder that we are ALL *so very worthy* of Her embrace.

Medusa Colouring Sheet
Arna Baartz

"It takes courage to dare to look at Her, to receive Her and conceive Her gift."
-Glenys Livingstone Ph.D.

If you enjoyed this book, please consider writing a brief review on Amazon and/or Goodreads.

We LOVE photos of our readers with Girl God Books!

Tag @girlgodbooks on social media – or email them to support@girlgod.org.

List of Contributors

Alyscia Cunningham is the owner of Uprising Builders, LLC—as well as an author, filmmaker and an accomplished photographer— who has contributed to such outlets as *National Geographic, Discovery Channel, America Online* and the Smithsonian Institution. Her work has been featured in *The Huffington Post, Cosmopolitan, Soul Pancake, Women, Action, & the Media, Proud 2B Me* along with other platforms.

In September 2013, Alyscia published her first book, *Feminine Transitions: A Photographic Celebration of Natural Beauty* and is currently working on her second book and documentary titled *I Am More Than My Hair: Bald and Beautiful Me.* Both books are Social-Change Photography Book projects.

Alyscia's specializes in promoting our natural beauty and because she believes the media does a good job of focusing on our insecurities and the bombardment of ads in the media proclaiming that their appearance without enhancements is inadequate or faulty. Her portraits are unaltered by Photoshop and reveal women as they are naturally, without the facade they put on for others. Alyscia is a master of her craft, and her calm and opened personality allows her clients to open up and show their inner selves.

Angela Kunschmann is an ordained Priestess at Mother Grove Goddess Temple of Asheville, NC and a proud devotee of Freyja. She enjoys a close relationship with Mother Mary, Frau Holle, Baba Yaga and Heimdall. She also teaches various workshops at Raven & Crone in Asheville, NC and is preparing to volunteer at the hospital to sit vigil with the lonely and dying. In her spare time, she enjoys outdoor sports and hiking with her 3 children, and knits.

Arna Baartz (cover artist and contributor) is a painter, writer/poet, martial artist, educator and mother to eight fantastic children. She has been expressing herself creatively for more than 40 years and finds it to be her favourite way of exploring her inner being enough to evolve positively in an externally-focused world. Arna's artistic and literary expression is her creative perspective of the stories she observes playing out around her. Claims to fame: Arna has been selected for major art prizes and won a number of awards, published many books, and— (her favourite) was being used as a 'paintbrush' at the age of two by well-known Australian artist John Olsen. Arna lives and works from her bush studio in the Northern Rivers, NSW Australia. Her website is arnabaartz.com.au.

Barbara Ardinger, Ph.D. (www.barbaraardinger.com) is the author of *Pagan Every Day, Finding New Goddesses, Practicing the Presence of the Goddess, Goddess Meditations*, and two novels, *Secret Lives* and *Quicksilver Moon*. Her blogs appear every month on her website and on *Feminism and Religion*, where she is a regular Pagan contributor. She has been writing for the Llewellyn annuals since 2004, and her work has also been published in devotionals to Isis, Athena, and Brigid. Barbara's day job is freelance editing for people who have good ideas but don't want to embarrass themselves in print. To date, she has edited more than 300 books, both fiction and nonfiction, on a wide range of topics. She lives in Long Beach, California with her two rescued Maine coon cats, Schroedinger and Heisenberg. Her doctorate is in English.

As an artist, author and scholar, **Barbara C. Daughter** is exploring how combining intentional creativity with Goddess images can root women in ancient cultural wisdom from diverse cultures, as she encourages women's empowerment to transform themselves and their communities. Currently training to become an Intentional Creativity Coach, using the Color of Woman™ method, she intends to work with women individually and in groups to paint themselves anew. Her approach to the Numinous is varied, while always rooted in connection to our planet, Mother Earth. Barbara can be reached at embodiedlifecoach@gmail.com

In a former life, **Bonnie Odiorne, Ph.D., AW** thrived as an academic. With a Ph.D. from the Johns Hopkins University in French and Critical Theory, she was an Assistant Professor of French at the University of California at Berkeley. For good and noble reasons she decided on a career in community education, creating career preparation programs in basic literacy and ESL with basic computer literacy. She has worked as a writing coach and associate professor in multiple areas, online and on ground. She embraces her wisdom years deepening in wisdom spirituality and the divine feminine. The AW stands for Associate of Wisdom, affiliated with the Daughters of Wisdom. She has an article published in *Jesus, Mohammed and the Goddess* and has published meditations on the website Fire in our Hearts. She blogs on WordPress as bonniesophia at the Marginal Way. She longs to visit her stepdaughters in Georgia and Arizona, to see her grandtwins Elizavetta and Ethan, and to travel to beloved spiritual thin places in Scotland and France with her husband and soulmate. For now, she is a resister working with a local organizing group. She might figure out what she wants to be when she grows up and become a Wise Woman.

C. Loran Hills holds a Bachelors Degree in Art History and a Masters Degree in Counseling. She's been a therapist, social worker and community organizer. She and her husband raised two beautiful daughters who are out in the world contributing successfully to society.

Retirement from the professional world has opened up new possibilities. When she's not writing or taking photographs in nature, you can find her spending time with family and friends, hiking, camping and riding her four-wheeler in the mountains, or traveling around the world.

Loran is an explorer of sacred realms and a guide on the spiral journey of life. Dancing in the still point, she's becoming a wise woman one season at a time. She's the sparkling dewdrop on a leaf, the song of a meadowlark and the sound of trees blowing in the wind.

Website: http://loranhills.com/
Facebook: https://www.facebook.com/loran.hills
Instagram: https://www.instagram.com/loranhills
Twitter: https://twitter.com/fromLoransHeart

Caroline Alkonost is a young, enthusiastic woman starting out on her journey in the art world—inspired by Romanticism, Art Nouveau, vintage book illustration, society and her own witchcraft practice. Her art embodies all that is legend, lore, and magic. All brought to life through various drawing mediums, collage, textile, linocut and woodcut printmaking. Caroline is currently studying for a Bachelor of Fine Arts and resides in Sydney, Australia. She aspires to create art that ignites a sense of magic and wonder that revitalises the spirit disillusioned with urban life. Her art is also inclusive of diversity and reflects the situations and aspects of today's society.

Cristina Biaggi, Ph.D.'s latest work has been both abstract and realistic. Her sculptures, commissioned classical portraits usually cast in bronze, seek to portray the person or animal's personality—their soul—in one moment in time. As Ms. Chris McGrath, Director of Sales at Polich Tallix Fine Art Foundry says, "Cristina Biaggi is one of the most talented figurative sculptors we have worked for. She is highly professional and extremely interested in the precise conveyance of her original detail throughout the casting process. She skillfully captures the essence of her subject in her art, whether the subject is an adult, child or animal. Her work is truly beautiful." Biaggi's collages—both big commissioned pieces and smaller works—are expressionistically abstract and reflect a mood or a feeling. Large commissioned pieces such as THE RIVER and OCEAN were created on canvas, smaller works on paper using India ink, house paint and fine art acrylic paint.
http://cristinabiaggi.com

Dawn Glinski is a practicing astrologer based out of Lockport NY. She can be reached at www.6oclockastrology.com.

Diane Goldie is a feminist artist, working mostly in textiles, but is also known for conceptual paintings and portraiture, radical crochet, poetry and songwriting. Born in the Midlands, UK in 1964, she emigrated to South Africa as an 11-year-old where she received her secondary education in art education and her interest in social justice issues (apartheid South Africa would do that). Returning to the UK when she was 22 , Diane settled in London and focused on raising her family of two daughters before starting her own one-woman children's entertainment company that ran successfully for 25 years until the death of her father made her reevaluate life and decide to live and work as an artist. Now she makes wearable art that is worn by unique individuals all over the world and has a viral video on StyleLikeU that has her talking about her life and inspiring other women to be their authentic selves.

Elizabeth Oakes Ph.D., Vanderbilt University. Ms. Oakes is a retired professor of Shakespeare and American Women Poets. She is the winner of the 2004 Pearl Poetry Prize and author of 5 books of poetry. "Medusa" originally appeared in *Matrix of the Mothers.*

Dr. Gillian M. E. Alban is Assistant Professor at Istanbul Aydın University, Turkey. She writes largely on women writers from the nineteenth to the twentieth century, as well as on Shakespeare. Her book, *Melusine the Serpent Goddess in A. S. Byatt's Possession and in Mythology* (Lexington 2003), exemplifies her work on women in literature through an archetypal, mythic perspective. Her current book project entitled *The Medusa Gaze in Contemporary Women's Fiction: Petrifying, Maternal and Redemptive* is scheduled for publication later this year by Cambridge Scholars Publishing.

Glenys Livingstone, Ph.D. (editor and contributor) has been on a Goddess path since 1979. She is the author of *PaGaian Cosmology: Re-inventing Earth-based Goddess Religion*, which fuses the indigenous traditions of Old Europe with scientific theory, feminism and a poetic relationship with place. She lives in the Blue Mountains Australia where she has facilitated Seasonal ceremony, taught classes, and mentored apprentices. In 2014, Glenys co-facilitated the Mago Pilgrimage to Korea with Dr. Helen Hwang. Glenys is a contributor to *Goddessses in World Culture* edited by Patricia Monaghan (2011), and to *Foremothers of the Women's Sprituality Movement* edited by Miriam Robbins Dexter and Vicki Noble (2015). She recently produced PaGaian Cosmology Meditations CDs, and teaches a year-long on-line course "Celebrating Cosmogenesis in the Wheel of the Year." Her book and CDs are available at her website http://pagaian.org

Jack K. Jeansonne rented a room in a house that Marija Krstic was managing in North Hollywood while studying character animation at California Institute of the Arts in Santa Clarita. At that time, Marija played the guitar, sang and composed in a band called "Abyss" that rehearsed in the garage. The drummer, Lane, who was Marija's boyfriend, took a photo of her one morning and gave it to Jack, asking him to illustrate a Medusa image that she could use as a logo based on the photo with guitar necks and snakes. Marija has been using his illustration ever since.

Jane Meredith is an author and ritualist who lives in the Blue Mountains outside Sydney, Australia. Her books include *Journey to the Dark Goddess, Circle of Eight: Creating Magic for Your Place on Earth* and *Aspecting the Goddess* (forthcoming). She presents workshops and distance courses worldwide. Her website is: www.janemeredith.com

Janet Guastavino is a video curriculum developer by trade and a poet for the love of it. She received her B.A. from UC Berkeley in an Individual Major (Women's and Ethnic Studies), which she has found enriching throughout her adult life. Janet has been published in a quarterly newsletter distributed by advocates for domestic violence survivors and in an eclectic e-zine. She is descended from a long line of musicians, poets, writers, and scoundrels, and hopes she does all their memories justice in her poetry.

Jeanne K. Raines is a sometimes artist who has been caught by Medusa; she is also a Licensed Mental Health Counselor and retired massage therapist near Fort Wayne, Indiana.

Joan Marler is the Founder and Executive Director of the Institute of Archaeomythology, an international organization promoting archaeomythological scholarship. She is the editor of *The Civilization of the Goddess* by Marija Gimbutas (1991), *From the Realm of the Ancestors: An Anthology in Honor of Marija Gimbutas* (1997), *The Journal of Archaeomythology* (2005-present), *The Danube Script* (2008), and other publications. She is completing her doctorate in Philosophy and Religion with an emphasis in Women's Spirituality at the California Institute of Integral Studies in San Francisco where she has been an adjunct professor. Joan lectures internationally on the life and work of Marija Gimbutas and is the author of more than thirty published articles including a biographical article about Marija Gimbutas in Notable American Women, A Biographical Dictionary (Harvard University Press, 2004). Joan is the author of "An Archaeomythological Investigation of the Gorgon" in ReVision 25, no. 1 (Summer 2002): 15-23; and "The Gorgon Medusa" in Women in World Religions (ABC-CLIO, forthcoming).

Kaalii Cargill (I, SS, SWA, SN, SEAR) lives and works in Melbourne, Australia. She has been engaged for 40 years in women's consciousness raising groups, home birth, attachment parenting, parent-run schooling, psychotherapy, dream work, women's circles, and sacred ritual space. In the 1980s she co-developed Soul Centred Psychotherapy, a therapeutic modality based on the feminine principle. Her Ph.D. explored women's reproductive autonomy. She has 5 books available on Amazon, including *Don't Take It lying Down: Life According to the Goddess*, a non-fiction book based on her Ph.D., and *Daughters of Time*, a visionary/herstorical novel tracing a line of daughters through 4000 years from ancient Sumer to the present day.
www.kairoscentre.com

Kerryn Coombs-Valeontis is a teacher, art therapist and eco/nature therapist in Sydney Australia. She writes poetry and is often intrigued by the mythological influences and inspirations on people that are archetypal and universal. Medusa continues to be a character that helps her understand her own anger and rage; and explore injustice and redemption—strong themes she explores in poetry and art.

Laura Shannon has researched and taught traditional circle dances for more than thirty years and is considered to be one of the 'grandmothers' of the worldwide Sacred / Circle Dance movement. Through extensive research in Balkan villages and wide teaching experience, Laura has pioneered a new understanding of traditional women's dances as active tools for spiritual development. Originally trained in Intercultural Studies and Dance Movement Therapy, Laura is currently pursuing an M.A. in Myth, Cosmology and the Sacred at Canterbury Christ Church University in England. She gives workshops, trainings and performances in more than twenty countries, and her numerous articles on dance have been published in many languages. She is founding director of the Athena Institute for Womens' Dance and Culture and a regular contributor to *Feminism and Religion*. In between her travels, Laura resides in Canterbury, Findhorn and Greece. www.laurashannon.net

Leslene della-Madre is a mother, "shemama"—shamanic spiritual midwife and death midwife, author, independent scholar, poet, artist, ritualist, former TV host of her own cable show, *Wildfire*, and holder of sacred female shamanic wisdom. She has traveled and taught in the U.S. and internationally. As both student and teacher on the shamanic path of awakening for more than 45 years, she has taught the womanist shamanic healing arts for more than 30 years. She is an initiate in the metis Paiute medicine tradition of Grandmother Mahad'yuni, and is an initiated daughter in the Nepalese lineage of Ajima, protector of women and children. She lived for nearly eleven years on The Farm in Tennessee where she apprenticed in health care and midwifery and where she gave birth to her two now grown daughters. Her groundbreaking book, *Midwifing Death: Returning to the Arms of the Ancient Mother* has inspired many people to revision death and dying from a Sacred Female perspective. Grandmother Agnes Baker Pilgrim, chairwoman of the Thirteen Indigenous Grandmothers says, "Leslene has an important message and many people need to hear it."

Liliana Kleiner Ph.D. is a visual artist born in Argentina and raised in Israel. She divides her time living and working in Jerusalem and in North and South America.

Liliana is known for her visionary oil paintings and her earthy woodcuts which convey her vision of the "Spirit of the Earth."
Her work is Visual Poetry from a Feminine Spiritual perspective.

Liliana creates her own organic hand-made paper, and had published two art books *The Song of Lilith* (2007) and *The Song of Songs*, Jerusalem (2010). She has produced art films—*Lilith and the Tree* (1993) and *Lesbian Tango* (2006) and works with Performance arts and dance.

In addition to her career as an artist, Liliana has a Ph.D. in clinical Psychology, and specializes in Jungian Dream Analysis.

Her work is in galleries and private collections in America and Israel, and can be seen in her site: www.lilianakleiner.com

Lizzie Yee is a mother and crone living in rural Pennsylvania. A bluegrass musician, she plays several instruments and started a bluegrass group compromised mostly of women. Lizzie recently became an artist when in 2014 her chronic illness took a turn for the worse and she had to sit or lie down a lot. She started drawing and developed her own style of feminist art. Yee recently published her first feminist art coloring book which was greatly appreciated by women around the world. She has begun work on Volume 2, which will be out in 2018. She is also working on a bluegrass art and coloring book.

Luisah Teish is the author of *Jambalaya: The Natural Woman's Book of Personal Charms and Practical Rituals*, and she co-authored O*n Holy Ground: Commitment and Devotion to Sacred Land* with Kahuna Leilani Birely. Her latest work is *Spirit Revealing, Color Healing: A Creative and Soulful Journey.*

She teaches online courses, facilitates conferences and weekend workshops, and performs in theaters worldwide.

Marguerite Rigoglioso, Ph.D., is the founding director of Seven Sisters Mystery School and a scholar/practitioner of the ancient Mediterranean mystery traditions. Combining her background as a university faculty member, spiritual teacher, writer, entrepreneur, channeler, and clairvoyant guide, she mentors others in cultivating their spiritual knowledge and bringing their own sacred calling to fruition.

Dr. Rigoglioso also teaches women how to be transmitters of sacred oracle wisdom in service to individuals and the global community through her Priestess of the Dove Oracle Training. She is the author of *The Cult of Divine Birth in Ancient Greece and Virgin Mother Goddesses of Antiquity,* pioneering volumes that unveil the mystery of divine birth as an actual priestess practice that has been taking place on the planet for millennia. To find out more about her mystery school, visit www.SevenSistersMysterySchool.com

Marie Summerwood is an author, teacher and composer of women's sacred music. Her chants help women remember the sacredness of women and life. Many of the chants on her first CD, "She Walks With Snakes" are beloved at women's gatherings and circles. Her second CD, "Step Into The River" offers several chants to specific goddesses, including Kwan Yin, Isis, Venus and Medusa. Marie Summerwood offers wisdom gleaned from the Spiral of Life. She teaches about women's topics, including the

sacredness of grief, and ritual emotional work with the four directions. A grateful apprentice to the force of Beauty, Marie welcomes its many faces. Ave Medusa.
www.Mariesummerwood.com

Marija Krstic was born in Yugoslavia, raised in California and studied guitar since early childhood. She earned a Bachelor of Fine Arts degree from California Institute of the Arts in Santa Clarita and completed the guitar program at Musicians Institute (GIT). Marija recorded an indie album of original music at age 16, and another album (CD) after Musicians Institute—and has played, sang, composed and recorded for many more projects. She has acted in musical theater, opera, TV and film. Marija currently plays the guitar & sings in three all-female tribute bands: Lady Zep (music of Led Zeppelin), Foxey Lady (music of Jimi Hendrix) and Lynette Skynyrd (music of Lynyrd Skynyrd) as well as solo and group performances of original rock and cover songs. Marija also teaches guitar, voice, piano, mandolin, ukulele and banjo.

Maureen Owen (www.lotusspace.com.au) is an internationally accredited coach and facilitator. She holds a Master's degree in Organisational Development and Training. For the last 20 years, she has worked as a consultant, change agent and senior manager in the areas of human resources and organisational development. Maureen lives in Brisbane Australia with her husband Nick and their enigmatic cat Stefan.

Concerned with the number of people (particularly the number of women) she encountered in her corporate work who were drained of energy and exhausted from the endless striving, Maureen grappled with ways she could provide a service that would address these challenges. And from these early musings Lotus Space was conceived to focus on the whole person and to support women to live unapologetic lives of passion where their individual uniqueness can shine through. Lotus Space, using the Chakra System as the guiding framework, supports women to embark on a journey of self-discovery to renew, rediscover and reawaken powerful aspects of themselves.

Maureen knows from her own experience, the power of working with the chakras and their capacity to return us to balance and provide us with an expanded and enriched experience of being alive. She believes that the chakras provide a profound formula for wholeness and the blueprint for the evolution of the soul that enables us to look at life with fresh eyes; to see beyond our conditioning that limits what is possible for us; whilst learning how to deepen the connection and relationship we have with ourselves.

Meg Dreyer is an American graphic designer, illustrator and photographer. She received her BA from Dartmouth College and attended medical school at Columbia University before choosing a career in art and design, and completing her MFA in graphic design at Rhode Island School of Design in 2008.

She has worked professionally as a graphic designer and illustrator and has taught graphic design at the university-level in the United States. During the academic year 2014–15 she conducted design research in Turkey on a US Fulbright grant. Her latest book illustration project was a Turkish children's book published at the end of 2016. She currently lives in Istanbul.

Miriam Robbins Dexter holds a Ph.D. in ancient Indo-European languages, archaeology, and comparative mythology, from UCLA. Her first book, *Whence the Goddesses: A Source Book* (1990), in which she translated texts from thirteen languages, was used for courses she taught at UCLA for a decade and a half. She completed and supplemented the final book of Marija Gimbutas, *The Living Goddesses* (1999). Her 2010 book, coauthored with Victor Mair, *Sacred Display: Divine and Magical Female Figures of Eurasia*, won the 2012 Association for the Study of Women and Mythology Sarasvati award for best nonfiction book on women and mythology. In 2013, Miriam and Victor published a new monograph, "Sacred

Display: New Findings" in the University of Pennsylvania's online series, *Sino-Platonic Papers*. With Vicki Noble, she edited the anthology, *Foremothers of the Women's Spirituality Movement: Elders and Visionaries* (2015); winner of the Susan Koppelman award for best edited feminist anthology, 2016. Miriam is the author of more than 30 scholarly articles and 11 encyclopedia articles on ancient female figures. She has edited and co-edited 16 scholarly volumes. For 13 years, she taught courses in Latin, Greek, and Sanskrit languages in the department of Classics at USC. She has guest-lectured at the New Bulgarian University (Sophia, Bulgaria) and "Alexandru Ioan Cuza" University (Iaşi, Moldavia, Romania).

Nuit Moore is a priestess whose work and temple serve the Goddess and Her return to the collective consciousness, focusing especially on the empowerment of women, the return of the Goddess temple, and the mana and medicine of her path and teachings. Although she comes from mystic traditions from both sides of her bloodline, she began her personal path as priestess in the Dianic and Wise Woman traditions, and is also an ordained priestess with the Fellowship of Isis. She is a lineage carrier and has walked the path of this work since her earliest memories. Nuit has offered classes and ceremony on female shamanism, women's red moon mysteries, the Dark Goddess, sacred sexuality, the trance arts, pharmakeia, women's healing arts, serpent/shakti power, crystals and crystal grids, ceremonial movement and sound and ritual theater, etc. for almost 25 years and travels frequently bringing temple and ceremony to festivals and communities. She has been a visionary and teacher of the menstrual mysteries and eco-menstruation movement since 1991 and is a long standing weaver of the Red Tent web. In addition, much of her work as an eco-feminist activist is in connection with her teachings of holistic menstruation and women's sexual health empowerment. Nuit is also a performance artist/sacred dancer, ceremonial visual artist, spoken word siren, temple arts empress, and founder of the Ishtar Noir Ritual Theater collective—and is the creatrix of Shakti Goddess

Arts (www.shaktistudios.etsy.com) which carries her ceremonial offerings, herbals, menstrual sea sponges, yoni eggs, crystals, sacred art, and some of her written work, including *Ragtime Revolution* and *The Ruby in the Lotus*. Her website can be found at www.scarletshakti.com and she is also on Facebook at: Nuit Moore, The Scarlet Shakti.

Pat Daly (editor) is a mother of three daughters and proud grandma. A published author/writer on career and job search issues, Pat lives in Portland, Oregon.

Pegi Eyers is the author of *Ancient Spirit Rising: Reclaiming Your Roots & Restoring Earth Community*, a survey on the interface between Turtle Island First Nations and the Settler Society, social justice work and solidarity, rejecting Empire, and the vital recovery of our own ancestral earth-connected knowledge and essential eco-selves. She is a member of the Celtic mtDNA-based Helena Clan (world clans descended from "Mitochondrial Eve" as traced by The Seven Daughters of Eve), with more recent roots connecting her to the mythic arts and pagan traditions of both England and Scotland. She lives in the countryside on the outskirts of Peterborough, Canada on a hilltop with views reaching for miles in all directions. Her website is www.stonecirclepress.com

Penny-Anne Beaudoin earned a Master's Degree in Pastoral Ministry in 1997 and has published articles pertaining to religion and spirituality in several Canadian and American journals. She was nominated for the Canadian Church Press Award in 2000. Her fiction has been published in *Lorraine and James, Writers On Line, Ascent Aspirations, Flash Me, FreeFall Magazine, The Rose & Thorn, Skive Magazine, The Canadian Writers' Journal,* and *flashquake*. She was nominated for the Push Cart Prize in 2005. Her poetry has appeared in *The Windsor Review, On Spec Magazine, Quantum Muse, Room of One's Own, Les Bonnes Fees, Membra Disjecta, Offside,* and *Doorways Magazine*. She was nominated for the Rhysling Award for the year's best speculative poetry in 2009. Both her short stories and poems have won or placed in a variety of competitions. *holy cards: dead women talking* is her first book publication. She has submitted her second poetry manuscript to a publisher and is trying to remain calm and detached as she waits for the verdict. Penny-Anne lives in Southwest Ontario, Canada, with her husband Tony and various figments of her imagination. She sings, has been known to preach on occasion, blogs about writing and life at www.pennyannebeaudoin.com/news-blog/ and tries not to think about the unfinished novel languishing in her desk drawer.

Sara Wright is a feminist, writer, naturalist, and ethologist (person who studies animals in their natural habitat). She lives in Bethel, Maine and Abiquiu, New Mexico with her two small dogs, and a dove named Lily B. She has been published in a number of books, and has two naturalist columns, *The Bethel Citizen* and *The Abiquiu News*. She also writes for *Dark Matter* and *Return to Mago*.

Sudie Rakusin is a visual artist, sculptor, children's book author of the *Dear Savannah Blue* series, and illustrator for established authors such as Mary Daly, Carolyn Gage and Patricia Monaghan. She is the owner of Winged Willow Press where she uses her original painting and drawings to create coloring books, divination cards, illustrated journals and more. She has also created the *Unwind Time* coloring app for iPad.

Being an animal activist and feminist, Sudie's artwork flows from what moves her: women, animals, the earth, color, pattern and light. Her art represents the deep connection she feels with these elements. Through her artwork she creates the world as she would like it to be, where harmony exists between animal and human, and nature thrives. Her artwork includes 3-dimensional oil on canvas paintings, paper-mache sculptures and pen and ink drawings. She believes her creations are the best part of her. Art is where she goes for refuge, replenishing, and how she pays homage to what sustains her.

Sudie was born in Washington, DC. She currently resides in Hillsborough, NC, in the woods, on the edge of a meadow, surrounded by her gardens, with her Great Dane, Fiona Fig, and Pitt/Boxer, Marmalade Moon. See more of her work at www.sudierakusin.com

Susan Hawthorne has been passionately reading, thinking and writing about women's mythic history for forty years. She is the author of eight collections of poetry, the most recent of which is *Lupa and Lamb* (2014). *Cow* (2011) was shortlisted for the 2012 Kenneth Slessor Poetry Prize and *Earth's Breath* (2009) for the 2010 Judith Wright Poetry prize. Other poetry titles include *The Butterfly Effect* (2005), *Valence* (2011), *Unsettling the Land* (2008, with artwork by Suzanne Bellamy) and *Bird and other writings on epilepsy* (1999). Her poems have been translated into Indonesian, German, Spanish and Chinese. She is the author of several novels including *The Falling Woman* (1992), named one of the Best Books of the Year in *The Australian* and a verse novel *Limen* (2013). In 2017, her novel, *Dark Matters*, a meditation on poetry, violence and imaginative mythic thinking will be published.

She is an Adjunct Professor in the Writing Program at James Cook University. In 2016 she participated in a blog for which she wrote a poem a day for year: http://project365plus.blogspot.com.au/

Teri Uktena is an internationally known Akashic reader who has for many years been providing readings and instruction to others in order to advance crucial knowledge of each soul's purpose in the new millennia. Having studied with her Cherokee elders to learn the medicines, ceremonies, and traditions of her people, Teri has gone on to expand her experiences by studying with elders of other tribes and other cultures finding beauty in their uniqueness and amazement in their wisdom. She works to help people change their lives, to help them achieve their dreams, find divine purpose, and achieve happiness through Akashic Readings, online classes, The Akashic Reading Podcast, and her weekly teaching emails. You can explore her work at www.AkashicReading.com. She is also a sci-fi and comic book geek, a Whedonite, and an unrepentant BrownCoat and can be found on Twitter @TeriUktena and on Facebook: www.facebook.com/teri.uktena

Theresa Curtis Ph.D. is an avid Goddess worshiper who lives in the mountains in the Pacific Northwest. She began her graduate work in her 50's, and completed her Ph.D. in Depth Psychology from Pacifica Graduate Institute in Santa Barbara, California. Her thesis involved Imagining Vulva into Consciousness—where she tracked the images of vulva over time, beginning in the petroglyphs of ancient Goddess Cultures. She has written for Goddess Pages under the name of Theresa Curtis-Diggs.

Trista Hendren founded Girl God Books in 2011 to support a necessary unraveling of the patriarchal world view of divinity. Her first book—*The Girl God*, a children's picture book—was a response to her own daughter's inability to see herself reflected in God. Since then, she has published more than 50 books by a dozen women from across the globe with help from her family and friends. Originally from Portland, Oregon, she lives in Bergen, Norway. You can learn more about her projects at www.thegirlgod.com.

Upcoming Titles from Girl God Books

A Poiesis of the Creative Cosmos: Celebrating Her within PaGaian Sacred Ceremony – Glenys Livingstone, Ph.D.

Sacred Breasts: an Inspirational Anthology for Living Your Breast Life – *Edited by* Barbara O'Meara, Pat Daly, and Trista Hendren

The Wisdom of Cerridwen: Transforming in Her Cosmic Brew – Edited by Emma Clark, Pat Daly, and Trista Hendren

Cerridwen and the Cauldron: a Celtic Tale of Magic – *a children's book by Emma Clark, illustrated by* Reti Toriella

Lady of the Forge: Stories and Art Dedicated to the Goddess Brigid – Edited by Isca Johnson, Pat Daly, and Trista Hendren

Women's Sovereignty and Body Autonomy Beyond Roe v. Wade – Edited by Arlene Bailey, Pat Daly, Sharon Smith and Trista Hendren

Kali Rising: Sacred Rage – Edited by C. Ara Campbell, Jaclyn Cherie, Pat Daly, and Trista Hendren

Pain Perspectives: Finding Meaning in the Fire – Edited by Kay Louise Aldred, Pat Daly, and Trista Hendren

Making Love with the Divine: Sacred, Ecstatic, and Erotic Experiences – Kay Louise Aldred

Rainbow Goddess – Celebrating Neurodiversity – Edited by Kay Louise Aldred, Pat Daly, Tamara Albanna, and Trista Hendren

thegirlgod.com/publishing.php

Want More Medusa??

Join us for the 4-week series, Medusa Speaks!

Hosted by Trista Hendren featuring conversations with Miriam Robbins Dexter, Glenys Livingstone, Joan Marler and Laura Shannon.

MEDUSA SPEAKS: REFRAMING FEMININE POWER

FROM MONSTROUS TO MAJESTIC
A POWERFUL CONVERSATION SERIES

A GIRL GOD PRODUCTION

Art by Kat Shaw

thegirlgod.com/ms.php

Printed in Great Britain
by Amazon